T N A M
ɪ THE WAR YEARS

SERIES EDITOR
David L. Anderson
University of Indianapolis

The Vietnam War and the tumultuous internal upheavals in America that coincided with it marked a watershed era in U.S. history. These events profoundly challenged America's heroic self-image. During the 1950s, the United States defined Southeast Asia as an area of vital strategic importance. In the 1960s this view produced a costly American military campaign that continued into the early 1970s. The Vietnam War was the nation's longest war and ended with an unprecedented U.S. failure to achieve its stated objectives. Simultaneous with this frustrating military intervention and the domestic debate that it produced were other tensions created by student activism on campuses— the black struggle for civil rights and the women's liberation movement. The books in this series explore the complex and controversial issues of the period from the mid-1950s to the mid-1970s in brief and engaging volumes. To facilitate continued and informed debate on these contested subjects, each book examines a military, political, or diplomatic issue; the role of a key individual; or one of the domestic changes in America during the war.

VOLUMES PUBLISHED

Melvin Small. *Antiwarriors: The Vietnam War and the Battle for America's Hearts and Minds,* 2002. Cloth: ISBN 0-8420-2895-1. Paper: ISBN 0-8420-2896-X.

ANTIWARRIORS

ANTIWARRIORS

THE VIETNAM WAR AND THE
BATTLE FOR AMERICA'S HEARTS AND MINDS

MELVIN SMALL

VIETNAM
AMERICA IN THE WAR YEARS
VOLUME I

SR BOOKS
Lanham • Boulder • New York • Toronto • Oxford

Published by SR Books
An imprint of Rowman & Littlefield Publishers, Inc.
A wholly owned subsidiary of The Rowman & Littlefield Publishing Group, Inc.
4501 Forbes Boulevard, Suite 200
Lanham, MD 20706

PO Box 317
Oxford
OX2 9RU, UK

Copyright © 2002 by Scholarly Resources, Inc.
First SR Books edition 2004

All rights reserved. No part of this publication may be reproduced, stored
in a retrieval system, or transmitted in any form or by any means, electronic,
mechanical, photocopying, recording, or otherwise, without the prior
permission of the publisher.

British Library Cataloguing in Publication Information Available

Library of Congress Cataloging-in-Publication Data

Small, Melvin.
    Antiwarriors: the Vietnam war and the battle for America's hearts and minds /
Melvin Small.
        p. cm.—(Vietnam, America in the war years; v. 1)
    Includes bibliographical references and index.
    ISBN 0-8420-2895-1 (cloth: alk. paper)—ISBN 0-8420-2896-X (pbk: alk. paper)
    1. Vietnamese Conflict, 1961–1975—Protest Movements—United States. 2. United
States—History—1945– I. Title. II. Series.

DS559.62.U6 S639 2002
959.704'3-dc21   2002021842

Printed in the United States of America

*For the patriotic Americans who served in Vietnam
and the patriotic Americans who struggled to bring them home.*

ABOUT THE AUTHOR

Melvin Small, who received his Ph.D. from the University of Michigan, is a professor of history at Wayne State University and a former
president of the Peace Science Society. He has written or edited a dozen
books including *Johnson, Nixon, and the Doves* (1988), which won
the Warren F. Kuehl Prize of the Society for Historians of American
Foreign Relations; *Covering Dissent: The Media and the Anti-Vietnam
War Movement* (1994); *Democracy and Diplomacy* (1996); and *The
Presidency of Richard Nixon* (1999).

Contents

Preface

The anti-Vietnam War movement is as controversial a subject as the war itself. Many Americans agreed with President George Bush when he castigated Bill Clinton during the 1992 presidential campaign for protesting against the war in London in 1969. But Pulitzer Prize-winning historian Joseph Ellis thought so much of those who opposed the war that he felt compelled to tell his students about his fictitious exploits as a leader of the movement. When the children of Americans of Clinton's and Ellis's generation ask their parents that age-old question, "What did you do in the war, Daddy?" they refer to the conflict at home as well as in Southeast Asia.

Considering the passions that still surround that most turbulent period in recent American history, it is incumbent on anyone who lived through it as an adult and who tries to write and teach about it to explain what he or she did in the war. I was too old and married with children to be subject to the draft, but I was a participant-observer in the antiwar movement, convinced that military involvement in Southeast Asia was not in America's national security interests. My wife, who was far more optimistic about the prospects of altering American foreign policy than I, was elected a Democratic precinct delegate in the insurgent movement supporting the nomination for president of antiwar senator Eugene McCarthy. We both attended many political meetings, rallies, and marches during the period, consumed by the issue that was tearing the country apart. Neither of us broke any windows, set any fires, or spit on GIs returning from the front. Like the vast majority of Americans who actively opposed the American commitment to the government of South Vietnam, we believed that our activities were those of loyal and patriotic citizens. And, like the vast majority of those who have peacefully protested against "Globalization" in recent years, we were angered by the violent revolutionaries, sectarian dogmatists, foul-mouthed chanters, and vocal supporters of the North

Vietnamese who gave our movement a disreputable reputation among the very people we were trying to convince to join our ranks.

All participant-observers of important events learn that with the development of historical perspective that comes only decades after those events have occurred, and with the increasing availability of archival and memoir material, things that once seemed so clear become far more complex. So has it been with my own studies of and teachings about the antiwar movement. Acutely aware of my once strong personal feelings about the war and the movement, I have worked hard to try to deal with those subjects as objectively as possible, recognizing, of course, that there is no such thing as completely objective history.

This is a work of synthesis. My narrative rests on the many fine monographs and memoirs that have been written about the war and the movement. I present the major activities of the movement and antiwar politicians and how they were viewed by the media and by the decision makers in Washington. I am interested not only in internal movement history but also in its impact on the policies of Presidents Lyndon Johnson and Richard Nixon. Further, I have addressed theoretical issues concerning protest movements in the United States that transcend the movement against the Vietnam War. These include the effectiveness of various oppositional tactics and strategies, the central role of the media in affecting those tactics and strategies, the way decision makers view movements, and popular perceptions of protesters, as well as the general question of the relationship between public opinion and foreign policy in a democracy. I have kept footnotes to a minimum, citing only direct quotations from readily available secondary sources.

I am indebted to Terry Anderson, Natalie Atkin, Mitch Hall, Ken Heineman, Frank Koscielski, Larry Wittner, and series editor David Anderson for their many useful suggestions about how to improve this book. In addition, Carole Le Faivre-Rochester did a splendid copyediting job and Nancy Berliner offered exceptional assistance in the final production process. Finally, my best friend, Sarajane Miller-Small, a veteran of the struggle for the hearts and minds of Americans, served as my muse and final copy editor as she has for all of my books.

List of Abbreviations

ADA	Americans for Democratic Action
AFSC	American Friends Service Committee
BEM	Business Executives Move For Peace
CALCAV	Clergy and Laymen Concerned About Vietnam
CIA	Central Intelligence Agency
CNVA	Committee for Non-Violent Action
CO	Conscientious Objector
CORE	Congress on Racial Equality
COSVN	Central Office for South Vietnam
CP	Communist Party
FBI	Federal Bureau of Investigation
FOR	Fellowship of Reconciliation
FSM	Free Speech Movement
FTA	Free the Army
HUAC	House Committee on Un-American Activities
IRS	Internal Revenue Service
LINK	Serviceman's Link to the Peace Movement
Mobe	National Mobilization Committee to End the War in Vietnam
M2M	May 2nd Movement
NAG	National Action Group
NCCEWVN	National Coordinating Committee to End the War in Vietnam
NLF	National Liberation Front
NPAC	National Peace Action Coalition
NSA	National Student Association
NSC	National Security Council
PCPJ	People's Coalition for Peace and Justice
PLP	Progressive Labor Party
POW	Prisoner of War
ROTC	Reserve Officers' Training Corps

SANE	National Committee for a Sane Nuclear Policy
SCLC	Southern Christian Leadership Conference
SDS	Students for a Democratic Society
SNCC	Student Nonviolent Coordinating Committee
UAW	United Automobile Workers
VDC	Vietnam Day Committee
VVAW	Vietnam Veterans Against the War
WILPF	Women's International League for Peace and Freedom
WRL	War Resisters League
WSP	Women Strike For Peace
YAF	Young Americans for Freedom
YSA	Young Socialist Alliance

CHAPTER One

THE ORIGINS OF THE MOVEMENT

"WE WERE YOUNG, WE WERE RECKLESS, ARROGANT, headstrong—and we were right. I regret nothing," proclaimed Abbie Hoffman, one of the more colorful leaders in the American anti-Vietnam War movement, the largest and most influential of all antiwar movements in the nation's history.[1] Although never able to create enough pressure on decision makers to end U.S. involvement in the war, it served as a major constraint on their abilities to escalate. Further, the movement played a significant role not only in President Lyndon Johnson's decision in 1968 not to seek another term but also in the Watergate affair that brought down President Richard Nixon. In many ways, the movement's greatest importance was its legacy. The unpopularity of the war in Vietnam among draftees and draft-eligible men led Nixon to call for the termination of the Selective Service System and the introduction of an all-volunteer army. Moreover, for a quarter of a century after the end of the war, as American presidents considered their responses to crises in Central America, the Persian Gulf, and the Balkans, they worried about creating another powerful antiwar movement that would oppose the interventions they contemplated.

THIS ANTIWAR MOVEMENT WAS NOT THE FIRST IN AMERICAN HISTORY. All American wars spawned dissenters, some of whom took to the streets, meeting halls, and newspapers to promote their arguments—starting with the country's very first war, the American Revolution. Although they never joined together to constitute a "movement," as many as one-third of colonial Americans opposed the break with England. Two decades later during the undeclared naval war with France (1798–1800), Congress passed alien and sedition acts to deal forcefully—and critics claimed unconstitutionally—with dissenters. The War of 1812 produced its own band of dissenters, including a sizable number of New Englanders who contemplated secession. To be sure, most Americans supported the war with Mexico in 1846, but after their forces failed to win a quick victory, opposition arose that ultimately produced a House resolution of censure against President James K. Polk for getting into the war in the first place. John Quincy Adams and Abraham Lincoln were among Polk's congressional opponents.

The Civil War produced not only northern Copperheads who schemed against the Union's efforts but also violent antidraft riots in New York City in 1863. During America's first anti-guerrilla war, the suppression of the Philippine independence movement from 1899 to 1902, a byproduct of the more popular Spanish-American War, many influential political, business, labor, and intellectual leaders joined together to denounce what they labeled President William McKinley's imperialist war.

A significant minority of Americans also opposed President Woodrow Wilson's call for entry into World War I in April 1917. During the year and one-half of that war, their spirited attacks on both the entry and the draft led Congress to pass another series of controversial alien and sedition acts which limited the opinions that could be expressed in the United States while the war raged on in Europe. In fact, the leader of the Socialist Party, Eugene V. Debs, who was imprisoned for flouting that law, found himself running for president in 1920 from his jail cell.

World War II, a more universally popular war, elicited little serious opposition, except from the small number of American pacifists who opposed all wars on religious or philosophical principles. It is interesting to note, however, that some clergy who otherwise supported the war effort did speak out in 1944 and 1945 when the Army Air Force began intensive bombings of heavily populated German cities.

Almost all Americans "rallied round the flag" in 1950 when President Harry S. Truman ordered American forces into South Korea, under cover of the United Nations banner, to oppose North Korea's invasion. Moreover, at no time during that three-year war did many citizens criticize the initial commitment to Seoul. All the same, after the new-style limited war became a stalemate in 1951, more and more Americans called on the president to bring their boys home. The issue of the "no-win war" helped propel the Republicans to electoral victory in 1952, especially after their popular presidential candidate, General Dwight D. Eisenhower, promised to go to Korea to see what he could do to end the conflict.

Despite the spirited opposition to these American wars, none compared in size, duration, and intensity to the movement that started in 1965, when the United States began to escalate dramatically the war in Vietnam, and ended in 1972, when almost all American combat forces had come home. Moreover, no other antiwar movement was as complex as that which aimed to stop American military involvement in the wars in Southeast Asia.

THERE WERE NO MEMBERSHIP CARDS IN THIS MOVEMENT, NOR WERE there any organizations that dominated its activities during the more than seven years of its existence. In fact, citizens could not formally join the movement as they might join a political party, labor union, or interest group. If you said you were in the movement, you were accepted as a member in good standing. You became part of an ever-shifting coalition of pacifists, liberals, social democrats, socialists, Communists, and cultural radicals, many of whom were college students, working people, suburbanites, clerics, politicians, journalists, intellectuals, and even proverbial little old ladies in tennis shoes. By 1969 there may have been as many as 17,000 national, regional, and local organizations that could be considered in the movement. Even local groups such as New York's Fifth Avenue Peace Parade Committee and the Chicago Peace Council were themselves coalitions of 130 and 30 peace groups, respectively. Although at first glance such numbers seem impressive, the movement engaged the active support of only a minority of Americans, with perhaps as few as six million participating in its major events and twenty-five million on the sidelines sympathizing with them. As we shall see, however, numbers were not always the key to the movement's successes or failures.

Some Americans "belonged" to the movement, even though they never went to a demonstration or signed a petition, and others devoted all of their free time to licking envelopes, leafleting, and attending interminable meetings. The amorphous, decentralized, and often anarchic nature of the movement was both its strength and weakness. On the one hand, because most major antiwar activities involved ephemeral mass coalitions under whose banner everyone was welcome, they were able to turn out hundreds of thousands of foot soldiers in their war against war. On the other hand, because everyone was welcome, the media, which brought the movement's message to the public and administrations alike, frequently concentrated their cameras and stories on the most colorful—and violent and bizarre—of the protesters. In addition, because the coalitions included people and organizations with dramatically different long-range strategies and short-range tactical preferences, a good deal of the movement's strength was dissipated in internecine political warfare. Of course, the ad hoc, messy, organizational structure of the movement made it more difficult for U.S. government intelligence agencies to penetrate its leadership cadres.

Americans who participated actively, or even vicariously, in the movement were all united in their opposition to their nation's intervention in the war between North and South Vietnam. But they came to that position for a variety of reasons. Many, perhaps the vast majority, opposed the war on moral grounds. Others looked at it primarily as strategically unsound in terms of American national security interests. Still others saw the development of an opposition to an increasingly unpopular war as the stepping stone toward reforming American foreign policy, or destroying American "imperialism" in particular, or changing the political and economic system in general. Finally, although it is impossible to measure, a good number of participants in the movement were also personally concerned about the draft and the possibility that they or their loved ones would end up fighting in Vietnam.

Many in the movement's leadership brought with them rich experiences from other antiwar, human rights, and political struggles. Some had been longtime members of small political sectarian groups. Their years of organizing and fund-raising, as well as their all-consuming dedication to full-time activism, gave them a centrality in the antiwar movement far disproportionate to their numbers. From that position, they were able to introduce their agendas and philosophies to millions of relatively apolitical citizens who had never heard of them and their earlier exploits.

Peace groups were among those in the leadership of the antiwar movement with the most illustrious and venerable histories. The Fellowship of Reconciliation (FOR) was founded in England in 1914 by opponents of World War I, most of them religious pacifists who assisted conscientious objectors. The American Friends Service Committee (AFSC), organized in 1917, a Quaker-based group also concerned with conscientious objectors, soon broadened its agenda to other humanitarian issues. Six years later the War Resisters League (WRL) took up the struggle against war, moving beyond individual conscientious objection to collective action. Many of those involved in these groups were radical pacifists who not only supported conscientious objectors but also called for more direct action against warring governments, including the use of non-violent civil disobedience.

Founded in 1919 with a broader agenda than other pacifist groups that developed out of World War I, the Women's International League for Peace and Freedom (WILPF), which called for disarmament and peaceful resolution of disputes, was the largest of the organizations, with a membership of close to 50,000 during the 1930s. However, by the 1950s, although it still maintained chapters in sixteen countries, WILPF could claim only 4,500 American members.

During and after World War II the struggle against segregation led to the formation of a second round of groups and institutions that would play a major role in the anti-Vietnam War movement. The Congress on Racial Equality (CORE), established in 1942 primarily by members of FOR, employed tactics of non-violent civil disobedience in its struggle against segregation, tactics that would be appropriated by the peace movement. Although the antiwar movement was primarily a white movement, a few African-American leaders such as Dr. Martin Luther King, Jr., did participate in its activities, and quite a few Whites, who later became antiwarriors, learned about challenging government policies through their work against segregation in the South in the fifties and early sixties. Many Whites worked alongside Blacks in King's Southern Christian Leadership Conference (SCLC) after its founding in 1957, and in the Student Non-Violent Coordinating Committee (SNCC), which first appeared on the scene in 1960. In the mid-1960s, when SNCC began moving away from the goal of integration toward black nationalism, many of its disappointed white supporters, no longer welcome in the field, began turning their attention to what they viewed as another manifestation of American racism, the escalating war in Southeast Asia.

In the wake of the unprecedented devastation of World War II and the almost immediate appearance of Soviet-American tensions that had the possibility of leading to yet another, even more devastating world war, other peace groups soon developed. Devoted to curbing the arms race and improving international cooperation, the Federation of American Scientists was formed in 1946, one year before the founding of the United World Federalists. Both faced tough going in the United States with the vast majority of Americans uniting around their government's Cold War policies. Their lack of success spurred others to try new strategies and tactics, among them the Committee for a Sane Nuclear Policy (SANE) and the Committee for Non-Violent Action (CNVA), both founded in 1957. These two organizations enjoyed some success, with SANE creating a groundswell of support for ending atmospheric testing of nuclear weapons and CNVA popularizing that same cause by dispatching small groups of protesters into test zones in the Pacific.

Presaging later attempts to contest the "illegal" war in Vietnam through the judicial system, in 1958, Socialist leader Norman Thomas, scientist Linus Pauling, and British philosopher Bertrand Russell, among others, went to court to halt atomic testing on the grounds that such activities, conducted under the Atomic Energy Act, violated the human rights provision of the United Nations Charter. The courts were unsympathetic to their brief.

On the campuses in 1959 a small cadre of activists formed a Student Peace Union. Two years later, Women Strike for Peace (WSP), which would play an active role in the later antiwar movement, joined the amorphous antinuke coalition.

Many members of these groups, either individually or under the groups' banners, participated in antiwar marches and demonstrations that laid the groundwork for the anti-Vietnam War movement. As early as 1947 a handful of members of the WRL gathered in New York City to protest the Cold War and the Selective Service System by burning their draft cards. But it was not until 1955 that a series of events took place that now serve as markers for the movements of the sixties. On June 15, 1955, members of WILPF, FOR, WRL, and the Catholic Workers refused to take to underground shelters during New York

City's Operation Alert, a rehearsal for nuclear attack. The next month, Albert Einstein and Bertrand Russell published their correspondence critiquing the West for its rigid Cold War policies. On October 31, Allen Ginsberg, a leader of the emerging "beatnik" culture, first read "Howl," an epic poem attacking life in the fifties in Cold War America. Finally, in December, Dr. Martin Luther King, Jr., launched the Montgomery Bus Boycott to challenge segregation in his city.

Several other activities during the 1950s, the era of the so-called Silent Generation of young people, helped launch the activism of the next decade. Among the most important was the formation in 1957 of the SLATE party at the University of California at Berkeley, a forerunner of campus movements and parties devoted not only to reforming the university but also to energizing students to work for progressive causes outside the campus.

College students, who would be among the most important participants in the antiwar movement, were increasing their presence in society. During the 1960s their numbers grew from sixteen million to twenty-five million, inflated by the coming of age of the "Baby Boomers" who were born just after the end of World War II. On the college campuses, particularly residential campuses, young people found politically experienced leaders among the faculty and graduate students. A good deal of free time, and access to mimeograph machines and the family credit card, made it relatively easy for them to participate in demonstrations or campaigns at their colleges, in their communities, and in the nation as a whole. By the end of the 1960s, 20 percent of students polled claimed that they had participated in at least one antiwar demonstration.

In February 1960, African-American college students in Greensboro, North Carolina, staged the first in a series of well-publicized sit-ins to protest segregation in community stores. That same year, California college students took the lead in protesting against the witch-hunting House Committee on Un-American Activities (HUAC), which held hearings in their state, and also took the lead in opposing the death penalty in the Caryl Chessman case. (Chessman was a convicted rapist who achieved celebrity through the publication of a book that he wrote while awaiting execution.)

Such actions drew far more attention than two other events that year which had a major influence on the antiwar movement—the founding of the Young Socialist Alliance (YSA) by the Trotskyists'

Socialist Workers Party (SWP), and the more important transition of the League for Industrial Democracy's student organization into the Students for a Democratic Society (SDS). SDS became the most important New Left campus organization with as many as 100,000 members by the end of the decade. It was "new" because unlike the old Communist and Socialist left that considered the working class the main spearhead for revolutionary change, believed in the potential liberating force of modern technology, and which operated in an authoritarian and highly centralized manner, SDS spearheaded a movement that recruited college students, opposed authority and technology, and espoused decentralization. Idealistic, energetic, and confident, the young radicals believed, "We could achieve an egalitarian, free and participatory society through our political activities and insights."[2] The sophisticated old-left socialist Irving Howe thought that the SDS's founding document, the Port Huron Statement, was "a fresh exposition of an American democratic radicalism."[3]

While these organizations attracted left-wing supporters, one cannot ignore the influence in 1960 and 1961 of the youthful candidate and then president, John F. Kennedy, who inspired millions of liberal young people with his message calling for service to the nation. Many of the thousands of college students who accepted his message and joined the Peace Corps became opponents of American "imperialism" on their return to the United States. Kennedy took office at the time that another young leader, Cuba's Fidel Castro, began to attract the interest of radical Americans, particularly with his anti-imperialist message. Antiwar leader Jerry Rubin remembered Castro's chief theoretician, Che Guevara, telling visiting Americans who had entered Cuba illegally, "You North Americans are very lucky. You live in the middle of the beast. You are engaged in the most important fight of all."[4]

Although the 1950s and early '60s were generally perceived to be a period of conformity in which the mainstream media and most journalists and intellectuals apparently approved of the tone of politics and culture, the intellectual world did harbor important influential critics of American society. Among periodicals were two old standbys, the *Nation* and the *New Republic,* and several new publications including *Dissent* and *Commentary* for the general public and *New Left Notes, Studies on the Left,* and *New University Thought* for college faculty and students. Among the authors who found fault with life in America during the period were Vance Packard, who wrote *The Hidden Persuaders,* which attacked the advertising industry; historian William A. Williams, who exposed the roots of American imperialism in *The Tragedy of American Diplomacy*; Rachel Carson, who worried about the environment in *Silent Spring*; Michael Harrington, who described poverty in *The Other America*; and Betty Friedan, who explored, in *The Feminine Mystique*, the suppressed angst of the American housewife. These critics and others offered important analyses of the problems in American society that lay beneath the surface of the "Happy Days" of the 1950s.

When the mass antiwar movement burst on the scene in 1965, it took many Americans by surprise. But, as we have seen, it had its antecedents in the many earlier marches, protests, and campaigns led by groups committed to integration, peace, and social justice. The experienced leadership cadres and foot soldiers were in place for the new movement. By 1964 at least 150,000 Americans belonged to peace groups, a number that had almost doubled over the previous year's membership totals. The following year, many of them would be in the streets, energetically opposing a once obscure war in Vietnam.

Most citizens, from Pennsylvania Avenue to Main Street, who had paid little attention to society's critics in the fifties, paid as little attention to affairs in Vietnam. From the 1880s to 1940, Vietnam, Cambodia, and Laos were involuntary members of the French colonial empire in Southeast Asia. As with the British, Dutch, Belgian, and other European empires, Americans expressed sympathy for those kept in colonial servitude by their oppressors but had limited political, economic, and cultural contact with them. This situation changed during and immediately following World War II when opportunities finally arose for most colonies to make their break for freedom.

As part of their attempt to establish their own empire, the Greater East Asia Co-Prosperity Sphere, the Japanese informally took control of Vietnam from the French who had been defeated by Germany in 1940. After the Japanese lost World War II the Allies approved of Vietnam's return to prewar status as a French colony. But the transition was not easy since in 1941, Vietnamese Communists and nationalists, led by Communist Ho Chi Minh, founded the Vietminh, a revolutionary front group based across the border in China. From there, they launched increasingly successful raids against the Japanese and the French, to the point where they became the dominant power in the northern half of Vietnam and proclaimed their independence in August 1945. After Ho failed to negotiate independence with the French in 1946, the Vietminh was forced to take up arms against them.

Since the Vietminh were led by Communists and the Cold War had begun, the U.S. government supported the French in a colonial war that it began to view as part of a worldwide campaign orchestrated by the Soviet Union to challenge the West. American policymakers, now confronted by the possibility of direct Soviet assaults in Europe and by indirect assaults against Western possessions through Communist-led or Communist-backed revolutions in the colonial world, ignored two facts about Ho Chi Minh: he was the most popular anti-French leader in the country and although he may have been a Communist, he was a Vietnamese nationalist.

During most of the period of the French-Vietminh War (1946–1954), Americans were unconcerned about their government's policy that moved from rhetorical support to considerable financial aid for the French war effort. As the war came to a close in 1954, the Eisenhower administration contemplated intervening directly to save French troops at their besieged outpost at Dien Bien Phu, but ultimately decided against a rescue mission. One day after the Vietminh overran the outpost, interested parties, including the United States, met at Geneva to resolve the conflict. The Geneva Accords, not formally approved by the United States, ended the French war in Vietnam, temporarily divided the country into two political entities, split at the 17th parallel, preparatory to national unification elections to be held within two years, and prohibited foreign intervention. The United States was not pleased with the accords because, from its perspective, they represented a major gain for the forces of worldwide communism.

In the weeks after the conference, as the process began that ultimately saw Washington replace Paris in the southern half of Vietnam, the issue of American involvement in Southeast Asia was not one that produced much elite or public controversy. In part, this lack of interest was a product of the rather low-key manner in which the United States decided to draw the line at the 17th parallel in Vietnam that separated Saigon's authoritarian, but pro-western, government in the south from Hanoi's Communist government in the north. Few Americans realized that when President Dwight David Eisenhower and Ngo Dinh Diem, the new president of South Vietnam, refused to participate in elections in all of Vietnam, as provided for in the Geneva Accords, for fear that the Communists would win, their country had signed on to "nation build" for the long haul.

Between 1954 and 1960 the Eisenhower administration sent over $1.2 billion in aid to Saigon, the bulk of it in military assistance to enable the South Vietnamese government to contain a small Communist-led insurrection that began in 1958. By the time the new Kennedy administration took office in 1961, the United States had 800 military advisers on the scene in Vietnam. As the insurrection, now led by the Hanoi-directed National Liberation Front (NLF) and its military arm, labeled by Americans and South Vietnamese, the Vietcong, increased in size and lethality, the president slowly increased the number of U.S. advisers to 16,300 by the time of his assassination in 1963. More ominously, newspapers in 1961 began referring to the Americans as "advisers" because many of them were going out on combat missions with their charges in the South Vietnamese army.

In 1963, President Diem's military forces lost more and more rural territory to the Vietcong, and at the same time they failed to contain turbulent domestic strife among their own people. Consequently, Americans finally began paying attention to the war in far-off South Vietnam. Diem's Buddhist-led domestic opponents contributed to this interest through the sensational tactic of self-immolation, burning themselves to death in protest against his tyranny. These television scenes shocked Americans who were even more disturbed when Diem's sister-in-law, Madame Nhu (Tran Le Xuan), dismissed them as "barbecues." Her husband, Ngo Dinh Nhu, was chief of the secret police and a principle target of Buddhist ire.

For much of the time the United States was in Vietnam the American media generally supported their government's position. The year 1963 was one of the major exceptions as journalists on the scene reported back home about the corruption, incompetence, and unpopularity of the Diem regime. Most of those reporting had no criticism of the original commitment to help South Vietnam resist the NLF. But they expressed a good deal of skepticism that it could be done under Diem, particularly as he was engaged in two wars at the same time, one against the Communists in the field and the other against Buddhist and other dissidents in Saigon. Such reports deeply concerned a wide variety of American leaders.

Among those in the United States who began to speak out against the Vietnam project were Democratic senator Mike Mansfield, an

Asian expert; influential columnist Walter Lippmann; political scientist Hans Morgenthau, who was once a member of the pro-Saigon
American Friends of Vietnam; pacifist leader A. J. Muste; civil rights
leaders A. Philip Randolph and Bayard Rustin; and the editors of the
New Republic and the *Nation*. Critiques from respected experts and
reference figures such as these in 1963 and all through the war helped
convince ordinary Americans that the United States did not belong in
Vietnam. Similarly, as the polls later revealed increasing support for
antiwar positions, politicians and other journalists were encouraged
to speak out against the war—knowing that growing numbers of their
constituents and readers approved of their dissent.

In March 1963, fifty-five prominent citizens sent an open letter to
the White House urging Kennedy to listen to the ideas of Mansfield,
Lippmann, and French president Charles de Gaulle for ending the war
through the neutralization of South Vietnam. Open letters to the White
House, publicized in the form of advertisements in newspapers, soon
became important tactics of the dissenters. Among other rationales for
this activity was the notion that if readers saw the sorts of respectable
and famous people who associated themselves with the ads and petitions, they would be emboldened to join the growing cacophony of
voices calling for peace in Vietnam.

At an Easter Peace Walk in New York in April 1963, called to
sympathize with the antinuclear weapons Alderston marchers in
Great Britain, several demonstrators carried signs referring to Vietnam and the WRL's David Dellinger referred to the conflict in his
speech. This peace walk may have been the first indication of the
attention some American peace activists were beginning to give to
the war. SANE, the chief sponsor of the protest, had urged participants to concentrate on the nuclear test ban, but, as would be the
case throughout the war, it was impossible for democratic organizations to enforce political conformity on those who showed up to
march under their banners.

Dellinger was correct. The war simply could no longer be ignored,
particularly the spectacular self-immolations that occurred during the
summer of 1963. In August, Vietnam as a peace issue appeared prominently at the annual Hiroshima Day events in New York; in October,
Diem's sister-in-law faced picketing as she toured the United States,
and that same month, the Friends Committee on National Legislation
organized a Vietnam Information Center in the nation's capital.

Yet because the United States had lost fewer than 100 military personnel since Kennedy's initial commitments in 1961, the war in Vietnam was still not a major political issue for most Americans. Moreover, the coup d'état that overthrew President Diem in early November made it appear, at least for a while, that South Vietnam's internal problems had been resolved. And when in February 1964 the new president, Lyndon Johnson, reassured the nation that "the contest in which South Vietnam is now engaged is first and foremost a contest to be won by the government and people of that country themselves," most Americans—and the media—put the little war on the back burner.[5] As for political activists, civil rights was the overriding issue during much of 1964.

To be sure, antiwar critics and demonstrators continued to appear from time to time during the first half of 1964. Democratic senator Wayne Morse of Oregon, soon to become one of the leading opponents of the war, asked the Senate eleven times in March to put itself on record for or against American involvement in Vietnam. In April and May, in one of the first cases of Vietnam-related draft resistance, ads appeared in two newspapers signed by 87 and 149 people, respectively, who announced that they would not serve in Vietnam if they were called up. On May 16, 1964, on Armed Forces Day, twelve men took one step beyond advertisements by burning their draft cards in public in New York City.

That same month, few noticed the formation of a new radical group at Yale University, the May 2nd movement (M2M), which was dominated by partisans of the Progressive Labor Party (PLP), a Maoist organization. The movement had grown out of a proposal by a member of Haverford College's SDS to send medical aid to the NLF. The founding of the M2M was one of the first indications that fringe radical and even revolutionary groups were beginning to develop at elite universities.

Students were not alone in speaking out. On July 3, 1964, A. J. Muste, popular folk singer and pacifist activist Joan Baez, and two Catholic priests Daniel and Philip Berrigan, among others, proclaimed an American declaration of conscience in which they related the war in Vietnam to the brutal French war in Algeria. Three days later, SANE published and sent to the State Department a petition signed by more than 5,000 professors who called on the president not to increase U.S. involvement in the war and to consider the neutralization option. The petition signers were prescient.

During the early summer of 1964, many of Johnson's key advisers had become convinced that the United States had to step up its activities in South Vietnam where the military situation for the Saigon regime was deteriorating quite rapidly. They were working on a variety of contingency plans, including a call for congressional support, when the Gulf of Tonkin incident occurred. On August 2, the American destroyer *Maddox* was attacked by three North Vietnamese patrol boats in international waters off the coast of North Vietnam. Two days later, reports reached Washington that a second incident had occurred. It now appears that the North Vietnamese did not attack a second time. Seizing on the reports of the phantom attack, the president ordered the bombing of North Vietnamese port facilities and then asked Congress to approve this action and future such actions in his Gulf of Tonkin resolution. This resolution, which endorsed presidential initiatives to defend American servicepeople and their allies in Southeast Asia, was opposed by only two senators, Wayne Morse and Alaskan Democrat Ernest Gruening. Ever vigilant for subversives, the FBI secretly gathered information on those who sent supportive telegrams to Morse.

The lack of congressional opposition to both the punitive bombing of North Vietnam and the Gulf of Tonkin Resolution, which could be interpreted as a blank check for the president (a gleeful Johnson boasted, "Like grandma's nightshirt—it covered everything"[6]) matched the public mood in the summer of 1964. Few Americans knew that not only was it unlikely the second attack had occurred but that on the eve of the first attack, U.S. forces were assisting South Vietnamese commandos in an amphibious sabotage mission in North Vietnam.

Only one thousand people joined Norman Thomas and Bayard Rustin in New York at Hiroshima Day ceremonies on August 6, 1964, to denounce the bombing of North Vietnam, and only 400 pacifists held a peace vigil at the Democratic National Convention in Atlantic City later that month. Most Americans supported Johnson's explanation of his actions and the Gulf of Tonkin Resolution. In the aftermath of the affair, Johnson's "job approval" ratings rose from 42 to 72 percent in the polls, and support for his Vietnam policies rose from 58 to 85 percent.

Nineteen sixty-four was a presidential election year and the Republicans had nominated Arizona's conservative senator Barry Goldwater. He supported escalation in Vietnam and appeared to countenance the casual use of nuclear weapons in such conflicts. Goldwater did attack Johnson's Vietnam policies, asking the president to explain the situation in Vietnam to the nation. In July, before the Gulf of Tonkin incident, he proclaimed, "Don't try to sweep it under the rug. We are at war in Vietnam. And yet the President . . . refuses to say . . . whether or not the objective there is victory."[7]

Goldwater scared many Americans, among them opponents of the war. Arkansas senator J. William Fulbright, who soon became one of the Senate's most outspoken and influential doves, shepherded the Gulf of Tonkin Resolution through that body because he did not want to do anything to help Goldwater, whom he considered a "Neanderthal" on foreign policy. Similarly, famed pediatrician and author Dr. Benjamin Spock, who would soon become one of the most prominent antiwar leaders, was one of the founders of the Committee of Scientists and Engineers for Johnson-Humphrey that went "All the way with LBJ." Even SDS advocated "part of the way with LBJ." In part because of Goldwater's perceived hawkishness, Johnson, who ran as the peace candidate who would limit U.S. involvement in the Vietnam War, crushed him in the popular election.

DURING THAT SAME FALL THAT JOHNSON WAS REASSURING THOSE WHO were concerned about the war, unprecedented events occurred in Berkeley that soon resonated on college campuses throughout the nation, the same campuses that would become breeding grounds for the antiwar movement. On September 23, 1964, the chancellor of the University of California at Berkeley, a university whose name became synonymous with radical activism, announced that an area on campus that had been employed for organizing anti-discrimination campaigns could no longer "be used for the mounting of social and political actions directed at the surrounding community."[8] His action led to a series of rallies and acts of civil disobedience that resulted on October 1 in the arrest of eight students. At one point, 7,000 students surrounded the police car in which one of the arrested leaders sat. Mario Savio, who had been a civil rights worker in Mississippi, emerged as the leader of the Free Speech movement, which kept the university in almost constant turmoil for the remainder of the fall semester. In a memorable speech on December 1, Savio railed to a crowd, about the "operations of a machine become so odious. . . . You've got to put your bodies upon the gears [of the machine] and upon the wheels, upon the levers . . . to make it stop."[9] He then led 1,000 students and campus hangers-on to sit in at the university's administration building. (In an early blending of the political with the farcical, the Free Speech movement spun off a Filthy Speech movement that demanded the right to shout "Fuck" on the campus.)

In the end, the Free Speech movement won most of its arguments about campus political activism, as the university's generally liberal administration and faculty revealed that the higher education system might be the soft underbelly of American capitalism. Savio and his crowd captured the spirit of the times on many large campuses where students felt their individuality and freedoms were suppressed by institutions devoted to turning out white-collar professionals to maintain American capitalism. In addition, many of these institutions imposed rigid curriculum requirements, maintained curfews for women students, and enforced dress codes.

Not all campuses experienced comparable unrest from the middle sixties through the early seventies, but most of the major campuses did, from the Ivy League to the Big Ten to the Pacific Ten. Those campuses were not only the most visible in the United States; they were also institutions where the establishment, including journalists, had attended and where they sent their children. Secretary of Defense Robert S. McNamara was concerned that antiwar activities "increased with the institution's prestige and the educational attainment of its students."[10] Soon, the key issue at those universities would not be free speech, curriculum reform, or civil rights but the war in Vietnam and the threat of the draft.

As the Free Speech demonstrations were winding down in Berkeley, SDS held a meeting in New York to plan its strategy for the coming year. The majority rejected launching a campaign around draft resistance because it was too radical. Instead, with some opposition to the tactic, the group decided to sponsor a rally in Washington on April 17, 1965, to protest the war. At the time, SDS hoped to draw as many as 3,000 people to listen to antiwar speeches and music. One drawing card would be the keynote address from Senator Gruening who agreed to appear at the demonstration. SDS also obtained the cooperation of the American Friends Service Committee to serve as a co-sponsor. Other antiwar groups, including SANE, WILPF, CNVA, WRL, and FOR, ignored the radical SDS's original call for the demonstration.

By the time that SDS met in late December, the Johnson administration had decided to escalate in Vietnam with a bombing campaign against North Vietnam as the first option. It was only a matter of time before the Communists offered Washington an occasion to launch that campaign. Thus it was that SDS, among the more radical groups opposing the war, was in position to control the first major antiwar demonstration.

FROM 1954 THROUGH THE END OF 1964, THE UNITED STATES SLOWLY, and seemingly inexorably, increased its political, financial, and ultimately military support for the pro-Western government of South Vietnam. Presidents Eisenhower, Kennedy, and Johnson, as well as most Republican and Democrat politicians, were convinced of the importance of defending the Saigon regime against Communists and others who threatened to overthrow it. For much of the period, except for a flurry of interest in 1963 and during the days following the Gulf of Tonkin incident in August 1964, American policies in Vietnam did not interest or concern most citizens. Peace organizations and radical sectarian groups did occasionally protest against those policies with rallies, demonstrations, and political advertisements. But most of these activities were far off the media's radar screen and, consequently, the radar screen of most Americans.

Nonetheless, the elements of a mass antiwar movement were already in place by the time that the war in Vietnam became America's war. Through the 1950s and early '60s, domestic opponents of American foreign and especially nuclear policy had learned about the tactics and strategies of organizing protests. Many of these activists had participated, often in leadership positions, in the civil rights movement. Perhaps even more important, a new anti-capitalist, anti-materialist, anti-imperialist counterculture had been developing on many major college campuses as well as in several urban centers, which were to become bases of operations for the new antiwarriors.

NOTES

1. Terry Anderson, *The Movement and the Sixties: Protest in America from Greensboro to Wounded Knee* (New York: Oxford University Press, 1995), i. Hoffman, who was a manic-depressive, committed suicide shortly after he made the statement.

2. Doug McAdam, *Freedom Summer* (New York: Oxford University Press, 1988), 19.

3. Irving Howe, *A Margin of Hope: An Intellectual Biography* (New York: Harcourt Brace Jovanovich, 1982), 293.

4. Jerry Rubin, *Do It! Scenarios of the Revolution* (New York: Ballantine, 1970), 20.

5. Thomas Powers, *The War at Home: Vietnam and the American People, 1964–1968* (New York: Grossman, 1973), 8.

6. Robert Dallek, *Flawed Giant: Lyndon Johnson and His Times, 1961–1973* (New York: Oxford University Press, 1998), 154.

7. Powers, *The War at Home*, 3.

8. Ibid., 31.

9. Robert Buzzanco, *Vietnam and the Transformation of American Life* (Malden, MA: Blackwell, 1999), 162.

10. Robert S. McNamara with Brian VanDeMark, *In Retrospect: The Tragedy and Lessons of Vietnam* (New York: Times Books, 1995), 253.

CHAPTER Two

THE AMERICANIZATION
OF THE WAR

O N FEBRUARY 8, 1965, LYNDON JOHNSON ORDERED BOMBING raids on North Vietnam in retaliation for a Vietcong attack on an American Air Force base at Pleiku in South Vietnam. The bombing campaign, first labeled FLAMING DART and after it became sustained, ROLLING THUNDER, had been in the works for two months. The administration was waiting only for the appropriate time to launch it. The rationale behind bombing North Vietnam was three-fold. First, out of military necessity; by bombing strategically vital areas of North Vietnam, American forces would make it more difficult and costly for Hanoi to send materiel and men to the south. Second, John-son assumed that the bombing, which would slowly move north from areas just beyond the demilitarized zone to the heartland of North Viet-nam, would inflict so much damage that the Communists would be forced to come to the peace table. Finally, the bombing would raise South Vietnamese morale by letting them know that they were not the only Vietnamese taking punishment during the war. The main reason for the bombing, however, was that the Saigon government was losing the war—something had to be done to turn the tide of battle.

For over a year, under OPLAN 34-A, the United States had been assisting small-scale South Vietnamese commando raids into North Vietnam, but these sabotage missions had never been acknowledged. Now the United States was openly bringing the war to North Vietnam. At the time, North Vietnam had not directly attacked the United States. Moreover, although they had sent several thousand regulars to the south to aid the Vietcong, at this point, virtually all of the enemy military actions involved southern Vietnamese. In response to American escalation, however, North Vietnam soon offered its own escalation by sending more army regulars south to assume an ever-growing share of the combat role.

WHATEVER THE REASONS FOR THE BOMBING, THE ACTION CATALYZED an American and international antiwar movement. The images of a modern air force raining down death on helpless peasants who were not engaged in comparable attacks on Americans took away the moral high ground from the United States in its battle to win not only the hearts and minds of its own citizens but also foreign observers. Never mind that the U.S. bombing was extremely limited at first and pilots were under orders to strike only at military targets. The number of civilians killed and maimed and the number of schools and hospitals hit in collateral damage would make it impossible for the United States to convince many observers again that it was fighting to promote humane democratic values.

When the bombing began, few Americans expected that it would last until 1968. Indeed, had Lyndon Johnson known that, he never would have agreed to ROLLING THUNDER. Thus, assuming that their nation had embarked on a temporally limited program, 83 percent of those polled approved of the initial retaliatory FLAMING DART raids. At this point, Lyndon Johnson was a popular and trustworthy president whose Vietnam policies were generally acceptable to most Americans. He also played down the seriousness of the situation in Southeast Asia. According to his national security adviser, McGeorge Bundy, he "was trying to have things happen with as little political debate as possible."[1] Secretary of State Dean Rusk echoed this theme, explaining that "we made a deliberate decision not to stir up war fever."[2]

At the time, and indeed through 1966, administration officials were most concerned about the reaction of conservatives to the escalation.

They feared that if the president made the war too much of a national-security issue, conservatives would demand to go all out to win it, and that could lead to confrontation with the Soviet Union and China. That Johnson was nervous about rallying Americans around the flag made it easier for the antiwar movement to attack his policies because he refrained from trying to sell the nation on the vital importance of involvement in the war.

THE BOMBING HORRIFIED—AND ENERGIZED—A SMALL NUMBER OF dissenters who became known as "doves"—one of the symbols of the peace movement. (In the aviary of the period, "hawks" were those who supported escalation.) In an amazing coincidence, the day after the FLAMING DART raids, SDS advertisements for the April 17 demonstration appeared in the radical periodicals, *Liberation* and the *National Guardian.* Three days later, 300 members of WSP and WILPF picketed the White House. On February 19, fourteen protesters were arrested at the United States mission to the United Nations, and the next day, 400 opponents of war, most of whom were members of SDS, engaged in another small demonstration in Washington. And on April 4, 2,500 clergy took an ad in the *New York Times,* with the headline, "In the Name of God, Stop it."

In addition during this period, Benjamin Spock, who had figured prominently in Johnson's reelection campaign, sent the president several strongly worded public letters protesting the bombing. The 1,500 telegrams received in the White House opposing the bombing by a 12–1 margin were even more troubling. Of course, people tend to send telegrams to the president to oppose and not to support a policy.

Far more sensational than any of these activities was the self-immolation of Alice Herz on March 16. In the first of at least eight such acts by Americans during the war, Herz, an 82-year old member of WSP and a refugee from Nazi Germany, burned herself to death on a street in Detroit near the campus of Wayne State University. Imitating Buddhist monks in Saigon, she made this ultimate sacrifice to call attention to her argument that administration explanations for the bombing of North Vietnam in a hastily produced White Paper sounded like the Nazi's trumped-up explanations for the Reichstag fire in 1933. The media paid little attention to her at-the-time unique self-sacrifice.

That was not the case on November 2, when Norman R. Morrison, a 32-year old Quaker, burned himself to death in front of the Pentagon, outside Secretary McNamara's office window. He was responding to a report from a French priest that civilian villagers had been burned by American napalm. He wrote to his wife in farewell, "Know that I love thee, but must act for the children of the priest's village."[3] The strong-willed and self-assured secretary of defense, privately a very sensitive man, later admitted he was deeply moved by this incident. A week later, Roger LaPorte, a member of the Catholic Worker Movement, committed the same act in front of the United Nations, explaining in a note, "I'm against war, all wars. I did this as a religious action."[4] These actions had little impact on the public in general who viewed such people as crazed fanatics, but they undoubtedly moved those who opposed the war.

In the wake of the bombing of North Vietnam, Lyndon Johnson was prepared for the protests and dissenting telegrams but not for the teach-ins that attracted attention during the spring of 1965. Beginning with this tactic, the antiwar movement constantly displayed a lively imagination in developing ways to promote its ideas. The movement, according to Chicago peace activist Brad Lyttle, was "a laboratory that tested theories about how public opinion and government policy could be changed."[5]

The teach-ins had their origins, in part, in the Freedom Schools of the civil rights movement in which academics offered lessons and lectures on race in America in extracurricular sessions—often off campus. Looking for a way to make known their strong opposition to the bombing, leaders of the Universities Committee on the Problems of War and Peace, a liberal organization founded in 1963, declared March 4 a national "Vietnam Day" on over 100 campuses where students, faculty, and community members would hold meetings to discuss the situation in Southeast Asia. University of Michigan professors, who had been in contact with Professors Otto Feinstein and John Weiss of Wayne State University where a successful Vietnam Day was held, came up with the idea of a teaching moratorium on the Ann Arbor campus. Instead of going to classes, faculty would hold special programs on the war. When the state legislature threatened to take harsh action against any professor who missed classes because of the moratorium, the professors proposed an alternate strategy, a teach-in of lectures and seminars to be held on campus—but in the evening and all through the night of the next day—so that no one would have to miss classes. Thus, it was on March 24 and 25, that University of Michigan activists conducted the first teach-in for an audience of 3,000. Scholars, generally but not always with expertise in foreign policy and Asian politics, presented the issues in plenary and workshop sessions.

Over the next few months, teach-ins were held on over 100 campuses. The teach-in at Berkeley attracted more than 20,000 participants over a 36-hour period, with an all-star cast, including Benjamin Spock, folksinger Phil Ochs, Socialist leader Norman Thomas, novelist Norman Mailer, and leftist journalist I. F. Stone. Although teach-ins would be held from time to time after 1965, this imaginative tactic made the news primarily during that pivotal year when the war in Vietnam was becoming an American war and citizens were first learning about Southeast Asia.

At the Michigan teach-in, a professor recalled, "One student told me that this was her first educational experience" in four years in college. A Cornell academic marveled at seeing young people "changing their minds in your sight" at his teach-in.[6] This remark was an exaggeration. In most cases, teach-ins attracted those who were already activists or leaning toward the dovish position. For this reason, teach-in organizers found it difficult to attract administration supporters to present their arguments.

There was, however, a national teach-in, aired to as many as 100,000 viewers on May 15 on the fledgling National Education Network, which gave the administration equal time. Originally, McGeorge Bundy agreed to represent the government, but at the last moment, the president canceled his appearance by sending him on a trumped-up diplomatic mission. Bundy did appear at a make-up debate in June, and although he did quite well against political scientist Hans Morgenthau, the president was displeased that he agreed to the arrangement in the first place. Johnson was ready to fire him then and there and, although that did not happen, Bundy left the NSC for the presidency of the Ford Foundation the following February. The more hawkish Walt Whitman Rostow replaced him, and one might argue that in this instance, the teach-ins were counterproductive in their efforts to influence officials who determined Vietnam policy. Rostow had earlier been removed from the inner circles of the Kennedy administration because of his hard-line approach to the war.

That spring, the administration dispatched "truth squads" to campuses to explain its point of view to the students. The teams of diplomats and military officials often met unfriendly and uncivil audiences who did not always give them a chance to make their presentations. Some students began adopting the view of Marxist philosopher Herbert Marcuse and his seemingly anti-democratic theory of "repressive tolerance," which contended that one had to protect society from those with abhorrent political views by denying them a public platform. They contended that "fascists" or "Nazis" like the Washington war-makers should not be given an opportunity to spread their evil messages. During the sixties, many radicals referred to their country with the German spelling, "Amerika."

While those on the left attracted attention with new tactics, the vast majority of Americans continued to support the president and his policies in Vietnam. Throughout the war, pollsters periodically asked Americans two key questions: are you for the immediate withdrawal of American forces from Vietnam and do you think U.S. involvement in the war was a mistake. At no time from 1965 through 1972 did a majority of Americans call for immediate withdrawal from Vietnam. During 1965, the largest affirmative answer to that question was 17 percent in the spring. As for the war being a mistake, although 24 percent thought so in August, it took until the spring of 1968 for a majority of Americans polled to reach that conclusion. Thus, in terms of the general public, Johnson and those in Congress supportive of his policies knew that only a small minority of Americans held views similar to the dovish activists who occasionally made headlines with their demonstrations, teach-ins, and petitions.

To be sure, Johnson's Johns Hopkins speech in April 1965, in which he held out the prospect of economic aid to all Vietnamese once the war was over, and his announcement of a one-week bombing pause in May were to a considerable degree bones thrown to those who criticized the bombing. Despite the speech, Johnson and his advisers were not yet overly concerned about the criticisms from the "Fulbright-Mansfield-Church school" and worried far more about the "Goldwater Crowd" who were "more numerous, more powerful, and more dangerous than the fleabite professors,"[7] a term coined by McGeorge Bundy, a former Harvard University dean. Some leading antiwar professors were philosophers, linguists, literary scholars, and even hard scientists whose foreign policy credentials were suspect. In April, Dean Rusk complained, "I sometimes wonder at the gullibility of educated men and the stubborn disregard of facts by men who are supposed to be helping our young to learn."[8]

Until the Vietnam War, most Americans supported the bipartisan political coalition in Washington that developed Cold War policies. After all, they reasoned, the government made use of the intelligence services and specialists who were able to make the most educated judgments about appropriate policies to pursue. When academics, especially those from fields distant from Asian history or politics, made headlines challenging the factual bases of administration policies, government experts derided them. McNamara told one group of pacifists with whom he met in 1965, "We know things that you don't."[9] He may have overstated his case. Although it was not known at the time, one accomplishment of the antiwar movement's "experts," many of whose analyses were later proven to be at least as credible as, if not more so than, those of the administration, was to demonstrate that intelligent people with access to newspapers, books, and magazines could offer legitimate alternate prescriptions for American foreign policy.

Almost all of the antiwar criticism came from liberals and leftists, with liberals by far the larger and more important group in the president's view. In 1965 and 1966, however, many liberal leaders were reluctant to speak out strongly against administration policies because they did not want to undercut support for its sweeping Great Society programs, the greatest reform project since the New Deal. Further, like the president himself, they expected the then little war in Vietnam to be a temporary diversion that would soon be over. The president delivered his stirring "We Shall Overcome" address to Congress in support of the Voting Rights Act on March 15, 1965, barely a month after he issued orders to bomb North Vietnam. When the president asked Congress for supplemental military funds in May, it meekly granted them. As Minnesota Democratic senator Eugene McCarthy later explained, his colleagues were behaving "like a garden society—just bring up a resolution and we pass it."[10] Throughout Johnson's administration, even though increasing numbers of legislators expressed their doubts and even outright opposition to the war, the president never failed to obtain their approval for military expenditures. He knew it would be politically difficult for war critics to refuse to provide the needed funds to protect American boys in Vietnam.

THE ADMINISTRATION WAS NOT ESPECIALLY WORRIED ABOUT THE FIRST major antiwar demonstration against the war—the SDS led April 17 event in Washington. At the time, few observers realized that this was to be the first in a series of bi-annual mass protests, generally held in the spring and fall every year, in Washington or New York, and for those on the West Coast, in San Francisco—all venues with large, local dissenting communities for whom attending a "demo" against the war, or racism, or sexism came to be a routine weekend's activity. Organizers did not call for demonstrations in the winter because the weather was too cold, or in the summer because it was difficult to mobilize college students who constituted a disproportionately large part of the crowds. In addition, demonstrations took a long time and considerable energy and costs to organize—two a year seemed sufficient for their purposes. Some antiwar leaders thought the whole tactic was a waste of time or a weak "surrogate" for serious grassroots political work.[11]

Most doves thought, however, that demonstrations were an essential tool in their kitbag of tactics. Above all, they were mediagenic events that helped to popularize their cause. Demonstrations also served as rewards for the faithful who had been laboring in small groups in their communities, by providing exciting peace "festivals" where they could feel that they were not alone and that thousands of other Americans from all over the country shared their perspectives. As a contemporary social commentator noted, "When all these people get together they begin to feel they are sovereign. . . . that they *know* they are right, and that they, in some way, represent the country."[12] Participating in organizing the demonstrations provided a rush in itself. New York antiwar leader Norma Becker explained, "It was adrenaline, it was a force."[13]

The SDS demonstration in Washington drew as many as 20,000 participants, a surprising number to its leadership who had hoped for 10,000, which was an increase over the December estimate of 3,000. The Washington demonstration was the largest antiwar demonstration in American history to that point. The actual number of people in attendance must remain vague since it was virtually impossible to count accurately the crowd at any large demonstration. The movement, the press, and the administration used human and mechanical counters and even, on occasion, aerial surveillance to establish their estimates, but attendance calculation was a most inexact science. Organizers always announced a figure from the podium; this figure was greeted with self-congratulatory cheers, although they knew it exceeded the number present. The administration, through local police officials or the Park Service, always presented an "official" undercount. One reporter explained that he arrived at his crowd estimates by cutting in half the number given by organizers; a writer sympathetic to the demonstrators doubled the police figures to arrive at his estimate.

Calculation of crowd numbers was not simply a parlor game. As demonstrations came to define the antiwar movement for the rest of the country, crowd size became a key to success. If the movement wanted to demonstrate to the administration that it was growing in potential influence, it had to attract ever-increasing crowds. Large crowds also legitimized the movement for observers at home concerned about the war but fearful of being in what could be perceived as an unpatriotic fringe group. To attract large crowds, the event had to be more than a march and a series of political harangues—it had to offer entertainment and also, even more important, it had to accept partic-ipation by anyone who wanted to attend. And therein lay a problem.

Although 90 percent or more of all participants at major mass demonstrations were peaceful dissenters who supported their political system, a minority held Marxist, revolutionary, or counter-cultural views and a handful eschewed even civil disobedience tactics for uncivil violence. The media, particularly television reporters, looked for the unusual and the colorful to make their coverage interesting. They were not especially interested in the short-haired, well-dressed, middle-class adult who made reasonable arguments about negotiations. Instead, they sought the person carrying a Vietcong flag or a picture of Cuban revolutionary Che Guevara, or the radical provoking the police to vio-lence, or the bearded, disheveled person smoking marijuana wearing a profane T-shirt or an upside-down American flag on the rear of his or her jeans. According to one journalist, the typical activist seen in the media was "a hairy, filthy, ragged youth with his arm and hand raised in an angry gesture [usually] with a single raised finger."[14]

The movement needed an ever increasing crowd size to demonstrate it had momentum, but the larger the crowds the more likely they would contain activists who did not reflect the views of the organizers or the vast majority of participants. And these would often be the ones focused on by the media, read or viewed by middle-class Americans trying to make up their minds about the war. Some observers reasoned, if those are the sorts of people who are against the war, then we must be for the war. They were helped in their thinking by politicians, more in the Nixon presidency than in the Johnson presidency, who labeled the demonstrators Communists or hippies or sometimes Communist-hippies.

All of these problems could be seen at that first major demonstration on April 17, 1965. It was organized by SDS, a peaceful but radical group, which proclaimed that anyone, even members of the American Communist Party, would be welcome at its event. That decision almost led a group of prominent socialists and pacifists to boycott the affair. At the eleventh hour, they decided to attend, reluctantly accepting the SDS approach that everyone was welcome inside the antiwar tent. The visible presence of Communists and radicals from the M2M group and PLP permitted supporters of the administration to claim that the event was Communist-dominated.

After meeting at the White House, the doves marched to the foot of the Washington Monument to listen to music and speeches. Entertainer and pacifist-activist Joan Baez lent her talents to the rally, as did Phil Ochs who, capturing the SDS ethos, sang "Love Me, I'm a Liberal." Among the speakers were I. F. Stone and Senator Ernest Gruening. Stone, the editor of a one-person, muckraking independent newsletter, took issue with some of his platform colleagues. He was a longtime liberal who had "seen snot-nosed Marxists and Leninists come and go."[15] SDS leader Paul Potter brought down the house with his question, "What kind of system" permitted "good men" to do such evil? He said "We must name the system. We must name it, describe it, analyze it, understand it, and change it."[16]

When the demonstration ended, participants marched to Capitol Hill with a petition calling for a new Geneva Conference to end the war, negotiations with the National Liberation Front, and free elections in South Vietnam. The petition emphasized that the United States was wasting precious financial resources needed to address domestic problems. Prefiguring future conflict within the movement, several hundred young people, ignoring the direction of SDS marshals, staged a brief sit-in on the Capitol steps. March organizers had specifically excluded civil disobedience actions from their program because they were perceived as too radical.

The media generally presented conservative estimates of crowd size, gave considerable attention to the handful of raucous counter demonstrators on the fringes of the crowd, and paid little attention to the contents of the speeches. Although the police arrested only four persons at the demonstration, the media focused prominently on this, implicitly suggesting that violence of some sort usually occurred at such events. Journalists and commentators would frame their stories in a comparable way in demonstration after demonstration during the Vietnam War era. Although the majority of them were antiwar liberals, they were simply doing their job, and in any event, as proper middle-class adults, they did not view potentially unruly demonstrations as the most effective way to register dissent.

Although SDS was pleased with the turnout at its demonstration, it decided never again to sponsor such an event. Instead, some members suggested launching a national movement to violate the Espionage Act of 1917 and to support draft resistance, but at its conference in Kewadin, Michigan, in June, the majority, opposed to centralization, voted to encourage local chapters to do whatever they wanted to do about the war. Nationally, SDS returned to its original task and strategy—to work on radical economic and political reform at the grassroots level. Tom Hayden, among other SDS leaders, later appeared frequently as a spokesperson for the antiwar movement, but he was speaking for himself not for the organization. In addition, a new, more radical, and less experienced leadership was beginning to take over the organization. This change ultimately led SDS to sectarian and violent self-destruction in 1969 and 1970. One of those leaders, Greg Calvert, admitted to the *New York Times* in May 1967, "We are working to build a guerrilla force in an urban environment . . . we are actively organizing sedition. . . . Che lives in our hearts."[17] On the group's decision not to continue as one of the leading elements in the antiwar coalition, one SDS official later observed, "We really screwed up."[18]

The demonstration excited another group of radicals, the SWP, who saw the antiwar movement as a way to recruit new members. As one of its leaders admitted, "Our position was to go into the antiwar committees . . . and propose they declare against both the Democrats and the Republicans."[19] SWP officials were often able to play leading roles in antiwar coalitions that organized demonstrations, in part because they were full-time revolutionaries who, with rather limited cadres, devoted enormous energies to the task of putting together national marches and rallies. Needless to say, liberals were not excited about the domination often exercised by leftist groups. At this point most liberals took more moderate positions than calling for the immediate withdrawal of American troops from Vietnam. Socialist leader Norman Thomas commented on the strong attacks against American society and culture coming from those directing the antiwar movement, "I am interested in peace [but it] does not require us to hate America."[20]

One of the greatest strengths of the shifting and amorphous antiwar coalitions that developed during the period was the ability to attract doves of a wide variety of political persuasions. It was also one of its greatest weaknesses because the coalitions devoted much energy to political maneuvering, often revisiting battles of the 1930s. This infighting was the norm in most democratic societies during the period. Characteristic, for example, was the situation in Denmark where one scholar talked about the "unstable alliance" between Communists and "pacifist-orientated Radical Lefts and Social Democrats" who "never learnt to love each other."[21]

As leaders of the various antiwar factions considered their next moves, the Johnson administration was considering its second major escalation of 1965—the assumption by American forces of the primary ground combat role in Vietnam. Bombing had not forced the Communists to the bargaining table and the South Vietnamese forces continued to do poorly on the battlefield against the Vietcong, and, for the first time, increasing numbers of regulars from North Vietnam. Despite the enormous significance of the July 1965 decision to take over most of the fighting, Lyndon Johnson played down its implications, fearing again to arouse hawks who would demand a full-scale commitment in Vietnam, risking both the Great Society and war with China and Russia. As with the bombing decision in February, he was far more concerned with the Right than with the Left. Joan Baez was not the top recording artist that summer; American thrilled instead to Barry Sadler's "Ballad of the Green Berets."

Johnson never expected that his decision would result in an increase of American military personnel in Vietnam in 1968 to 550,000 from the 60,000 level of the summer of 1965. He assumed that American soldiers on the ground combined with the sustained, ever-escalating bombing would bring the enemy to his senses in a year or so. His July decision resulted in more draftees being sent to Vietnam and a dramatic increase in battle deaths and casualties, two of the most important factors in the rise of the antiwar movement in the following months and years.

As he was considering his decision, ten members of WSP met with six North Vietnamese and three NLF women at a conference in Jakarta, Indonesia. One of the members of the NLF delegation was Madame Nguyen Thi Binh, later the front's foreign minister. This meeting was the first of many between members of the American peace movement and the "enemy" which took place outside the United States and even, as we shall see, in North Vietnam. American activists went to these meetings to explore ways to end the war and also, to some degree, to express solidarity with those whom they viewed as fighting for independence from the West. The North Vietnamese and NLF were able to use these meetings to assure their people that they had the support of many American citizens. By the end of the war, over 100 Americans had gone to North Vietnam, sometimes coming home with prisoners of war released personally to them. This sort of activity, which the government contested in the courts because it was illegal to travel to North Vietnam on an American passport, hurt the antiwar movement more than it helped. Most Americans, even those opposed to their government's involvement in Southeast Asia, viewed anyone who traveled to an enemy capital during wartime with a good deal of suspicion.

They also would have viewed with suspicion the several thousand radicals and pacifists who organized an Assembly of Unrepresented People in Washington from August 6 through August 9, 1965. Three hundred and fifty protesters were arrested for a sit-in at the Capitol, including David Dellinger, who was fined $300. Refusing to pay the fine, he accepted his thirty-day jail sentence instead. Among those arrested were counter demonstrators, mostly members of the American Nazi Party, who had thrown red paint at the protesters. They were fined only $10.

The most important result of the Assembly was the formation of the first major antiwar coalition organization, the National Coordinating Committee to End the War in Vietnam (NCCEWVN), which set up headquarters in Madison, Wisconsin. Among the groups in leadership roles were the Communist Party (CP) and its campus-based Du Bois Clubs, the Trotskyist SWP and its subsidiary YSA, and the Vietnam Day Committee(VDC) from Berkeley, whose main spokesperson was Jerry Rubin. Needless to say, they often spent more time contesting with one another for power in the coalition, than in trying to end the war. At a convention in late November, SWP and YSA tried to take over the organization by using inventive parliamentary and extra-parliamentary initiatives that in several cases came close to producing fist fights between their members and their long-time enemies of the CP. One non-sectarian observer found such behavior "demoralizing to the whole antiwar movement."[22] To be fair, the sectarians claimed that the bitter contests were always about the best strategy and tactics to adopt to end the war.

Throughout the war, the SWP was a major provider of parade marshals, leafleters, communications specialists, and envelope-lickers, with its small but indefatigable loyal cadre. One old leftist, explaining how tiny groups like the SWP could play such a dominant role in movements, contended that "coherent minorities, firm in purpose and ready to sacrifice time and energy, can gain far more political power than a mere counting of heads would suggest."[23] The party clung rigidly to its tactical and strategic programs, however, alienating many others in the leadership of the movement. The SWP advocated mass demonstrations as the best way to develop public pressure to end the war and generally opposed those who wanted to practice civil disobedience either at their demonstrations or on other occasions. They were almost always challenged by the CP and fellow travelers in what one Communist Party member later labeled "crazy" behavior—given the necessity for cooperation to find ways to end the war.[24] In addition, this split and others were exploited by the FBI through agents provocateurs in the different camps.

While the NCCEWVN was getting organized, other activists were putting together the Fifth Avenue Peace Parade Committee, which was to play a central role in demonstrations in New York City. Its original mandate was to counter the Fifth Avenue Armed Forces Day and Memorial Day parades. Norma Becker, a schoolteacher, was one of the chief leaders of this coalition but she never received the headlines and recognition accorded to male counterparts, such as her colleague in the committee, the revered pacifist A. J. Muste, or Dellinger, Hayden, and Rubin. In part because of their experiences with the male dominance and even chauvinism in the movements of the sixties—especially the civil rights and antiwar movements—many activist women left those battles to develop the modern women's liberation movement.

Considering the difficulties activists encountered trying to work together, it was surprising that the NCCEWVN's first major mass action, the International Days of Protest held on October 15 and 16, 1965, was so successful. In the largest series of demonstrations to that date, at least 100,000 people protested in a variety of ways in more than eighty American cities and several European capitals. In New York City, on October 15, outside an Army induction center and in front of television cameras, David J. Miller, a member of the pacifist-oriented Catholic Worker Movement, burned his draft card to the delight of 300 supporters. This was the first of similar well-publicized acts of civil disobedience against the Selective Service laws during the Vietnam War. It was also the first such act that violated a new law Congress had passed making a person guilty of "willful destruction" of a draft card subject to a five-year jail sentence and a $10,000 fine. In a related action, as part of the weekend protests, thirty-eight people were arrested outside the Selective Service office in Ann Arbor, Michigan.

At the same time, there were even more dramatic and massive antidraft protests in Berkeley and Oakland, California. On October 15, 15,000 demonstrators, mostly young people and university students, assembled in Berkeley to march to the Oakland Army Terminal to leaflet soldiers on their way to Vietnam. Because they lacked a parade permit, the police turned them back short of their goal. The next day, 5,000 people tried to get to Oakland, only to be turned back again by the police and their unofficial auxiliaries, the "ultra-patriotic" Hell's Angels motorcycle club, one of whom was heard to yell, "Go back to Russia, you fucking Communists."[25] Striking the same tone, albeit more decorously, the Democratic governor of California, Pat Brown, commented that the demonstrations "gave aid and comfort to Hanoi."[26] On November 6, in New York City, five more men, only one of them classified 1A, burned their draft cards in a public ceremony. Hecklers, who tried to extinguish the fires by spraying water on them, carried signs that read, "Thanks Pinkos, Queers, Cowards, Draft Dodgers—Mao Tse Tung," and shouted "Burn yourselves, not your cards" as they attempted to drown out the speakers.[27]

Antidraft activity was one form of antiwar protest that *did* concern the administration. If large numbers of young people resisted the draft and impeded the registration process, they could make it difficult for the military to follow through with its plans to defeat the enemy on the ground in Vietnam. Moreover, the need for draftees was increasing dramatically. The head of the Selective Service, General Lewis Hershey, recommended cutting student (2-S) deferments for undergraduates by 20 percent and introduced a new program in 1966. In order to maintain their status, all students not only had to have a C average but also had to score 70 percent on a general Selective Service intelligence test that was administered on college campuses. In the spring of 1966, 768,000 males took the test. This new hurdle led to many protests not only against the Selective Service System but also against the cooperating universities. Some professors began giving men higher grades than they earned because they did not want to be responsible for sending them to Vietnam. The most famous slogan of the antidraft movement, "Hell No We Won't Go," was first heard at an Atlanta SNCC protest in August, 1966.

From the start, the government took strong measures against draft resisters. David J. Miller was convicted in March 1966 for destroying his draft card and given a suspended sentence if he would accept a new one. He refused, was brought to court again, and sentenced to two-and-one half years in jail in April 1967. He had to be carried from the courtroom to his incarceration, resisting to the end what he considered to be an immoral authority.

The draft was not the major issue at the Manhattan centerpiece of the First International Days of Protest on October 16. At least 20,000 doves marched twenty-five blocks for a rally at which I. F. Stone, among others, addressed them. In the largest turnout of counter demonstrators during the war, 1,000 lined the parade route to hurl insults, and occasionally red paint and eggs, at the people they denounced as unpatriotic Communists. Almost all of the lawbreaking that day came from right-wingers, but newspaper readers could easily conclude that these sorts of demonstrations produced violence and law breaking. Even when there was no violence or arrests at a demonstration, journalists often included that fact in their lead paragraphs.

The First International Days of Protest was dominated by the participation of mostly young people from radical groups with radical themes. Needless to say, they did not receive a favorable reception in the mainstream press. Influential *New York Times* columnist James Reston was characteristic, saying that the demonstrators were "not promoting peace but postponing it."[28] The key for him at this point was the necessity for Hanoi, not the well-intentioned Johnson administration, to make the first move to the peace tables. He was gentler in his approach than the Jackson, Mississippi *Daily News,* which commented, "This is the time for police brutality, if there ever was one."[29]

The police were not needed at a New York Support America's Vietnam Effort parade on October 30. Twenty-thousand people showed up to march behind five Medal-of-Honor winners in a demonstration organized by a New York City councilman, the head of the Mineworkers Union, and the *Journal American*. During the same period, 16,000 Michigan State University students sent a petition to the president in support of his Vietnam policies. Michigan State was the home of the chairman of the American Friends of Vietnam, an organization that lobbied for the government of South Vietnam. This organization and others that would be formed under both Johnson and Nixon often received informal, under-the-table backing, direction, and even some financial aid from White House operatives. To coordinate the public-relations aspect of the war at home, Johnson organized in August a Public Affairs Policy Committee for Vietnam, which eventually evolved into a Vietnam Information Group.

The administration did not have to launch much of a propaganda campaign against the radical-oriented International Days of Protest. This was not the case with a November 27 antiwar rally in Washington organized by SANE, an effective liberal peace group. Reflecting the split and even distrust between the two wings of the peace movement, this demonstration would appear to be redundant and certainly an unnecessary drain on activists' energies, considering the previous month's protests. Thirty-five thousand mostly adult and well-mannered protesters turned up to hear actor Tony Randall and author Saul Bellow, among others, argue in moderate terms for an end to the war through negotiations. However, the most electrifying speech came from the left when the SDS's Carl Oglesby described "those who study the maps, give the commands, push the buttons and tally the dead: Bundy, McNamara, [ambassador to South Vietnam Henry Cabot] Lodge, [UN ambassador Arthur] Goldberg, the President himself. They are not moral monsters. They are all honorable men. They are all liberals."[30]

The media devoted somewhat less coverage to this demonstration than to those of the previous month and generally found it colorless and uninspiring. The antiwar movement had a problem it never solved. Journalists lavished attention on colorful and uncivil demonstrations attended by oddly dressed young people, but were bored with more decorous activities where adults in coats and ties delivered sober addresses devoid of revolutionary rhetoric or profanity. Those colorful demonstrations that received considerable space and air time disturbed the middle-class public whose hearts and minds the movement was trying to win.

Even at the restrained demonstrations, the media tended to focus on the radicals in the crowd. For example, at the SANE rally, several people were photographed carrying Vietcong flags, an action that Dellinger considered "senseless" and "inflammatory." He reported that observers in Hanoi had urged their friends in the United States to carry only American flags.[31] Since tolerant liberals or leftists ran demonstrations, it was impossible to compel those who attended to conform to their informal "rules" about slogans and signs. Moreover, the North Vietnamese were not that circumspect in their approach to American demonstrations. They often sent public greetings to the event leaders, who dutifully read them to their supporters, many of whom cheered enthusiastically the good wishes from Hanoi. Congresspersons, who were pleased to read those greetings into the *Congressional Record,* attacked the antiwar movement for its treasonous behavior.

No doubt, a minority of those who showed up for mass demonstrations supported anti-colonial and anti-Western revolutions in Asia, Africa, and Latin America and saw the Vietcong as their allies in the struggle against American-led imperialistic nations. And they were proud of it. An even larger minority might have been there for recreation. As one demonstration attendee admitted, "Protesting was a great place to get laid, get high, and listen to some great rock."[32] Carl Ogelsby admitted he was drawn to SDS because it "had the best parties, the prettiest girls. It was the sexiest show in town."[33]

The vast majority of those who participated in antiwar events, however, were primarily interested in the withdrawal of their troops from the civil wars in Southeast Asia. To call for victory for the Vietcong was to wave a red flag in front of most Americans. Many years later, Tom Hayden confessed that he and his radical cohorts were guilty of "Third World romanticism," the glorification of those engaged in the struggle for national liberation around the world, who allegedly had established political systems and a way of life that were preferable to those in the United States.

As 1965 came to a close, the antiwar movement had barely made a dent in Johnson's public support. Over half of those polled approved of the president's handling of the war with 30 percent expressing a negative opinion evenly split between hawks and doves. One of the president's aides was accurate when he informed Johnson that the movement was still a "cloud no-bigger-than on the horizon."[34]

NOTES

1. Tom Wells, *The War Within: America's Battle over Vietnam* (Berkeley: University of California Press, 1994), 41.

2. Ibid., 41.

3. Charles DeBenedetti with Charles Chatfield, *An American Ordeal: The Antiwar Movement of the Vietnam Era* (Syracuse: Syracuse University Press, 1990), 129.

4. Ibid., 130.

5. Bradford Lyttle, *The Chicago Anti-Vietnam War Movement* (Chicago: Midwest Pacifist Center, 1988), iii.

6. Anderson, *The Movement*, 124; Wells, *The War Within*, 36.

7. DeBenedetti, *An American Ordeal*, 104; George C. Herring, *America's Longest War: The United States and Vietnam, 1950–1975* (New York: McGraw-Hill, 1996), 155.

8. Wells, *The War Within*, 27.

9. Nancy Zaroulis and Gerald Sullivan, *Who Spoke Up? American Protest against the War in Vietnam, 1963–1975* (Garden City: Doubleday, 1984), 46.

10. Ibid., 42.

11. DeBenedetti, *An American Ordeal*, 356.

12. Alexander Klein, ed., *Dissent, Policy, and Confrontation* (New York: McGraw-Hill, 1971), 60–61.

13. Wells, *The War Within*, 52.

14. Mitchell K. Hall, *Because of Their Faith: CALCAV and Religious Opposition to the War in Vietnam* (New York: Columbia University Press, 1990), ix.

15. A. J. Langguth, *Our Vietnam: The War, 1954–1975* (New York: Simon and Schuster, 2000), 357.

16. Wells, *The War Within*, 17; Powers, *The War at Home*, 76.

17. Zaroulis and Sullivan, *Who Spoke Up?* 118.

18. DeBenedetti, *An American Ordeal*, 112.

19. Wells, *The War Within*, 17.

20. Robert Schulzinger, *A Time for War: The United States and Vietnam, 1941–1975* (New York: Oxford University Press, 1997), 228.

21. Soren Hein Rasmussen, "From Social Movements to Political Movements," in *Scandinavian Journal of History* 22 (1997): 178.

22. Wells, *The War Within*, 60.

23. Howe, *A Margin of Hope*, 74.

24. Ibid., 53.

25. Anderson, *The Movement*, 141.

26. Ibid., 144.

27. Zaroulis and Sullivan, *Who Spoke Up?* 61.

28. Powers, *The War at Home*, 88.

29. Anderson, *The Movement*, 145.

30. Melvin Small, *Covering Dissent: The Media and the Anti-Vietnam War Movement* (New Brunswick: Rutgers University Press, 1994), 34.

31. Ibid., 58.

32. Myra McPherson, *Long Time Passing: Vietnam and the Haunted Generation* (Garden City: Doubleday, 1984), 33.

33. Kenneth J. Heineman, *Put Your Bodies upon the Wheels: Student Revolt in the 1960's* (Chicago: Ivan Dee, 2001), 60.

34. Small, *Covering Dissent,* 59.

CHAPTER Three

BUILDING A BASE

O N THE SURFACE THE ANTIWAR MOVEMENT APPEARED TO BE going nowhere during 1966. Johnson maintained his approval ratings in the polls, attempts to unseat prowar Democrats in the bi-elections failed, and no mass demonstrations or other tactics attracted as much attention as the three demonstrations and teach-ins in 1965. The experience frustrated antiwar leaders considering the increase over twelve months in the number of U.S. troops in Vietnam from 185,000 to 385,000, and the number of battle deaths from 1,400 to 5,000, with no end to the war in sight. In 1966, A. J. Muste sadly reported that the "peace movement in the United States hardly amounts to a hill of beans."[1]

Part of the problem was a lack of central authority. As Charles DeBenedetti, the leading scholar of the movement wrote, "The movement could not be controlled, but neither could it direct. Instead, it expanded and contracted, advancing and retreating in reaction to a war which itself could not be controlled."[2] But the lack of a central authority could also be a strength. Throughout 1966, on the local level, experienced and inexperienced activists rallied, fasted, circulated petitions, resisted the draft, and attended innumerable meetings as they laid the groundwork for a broad-based mass movement that would become a force to contend with in 1967. Little things took on added significance. For example, one of the top popular albums of the year featured Simon and Garfunkel singing "Silent Night" as a newscaster offering combat reports from Vietnam and other disturbing stories became louder and louder, eventually drowning out the Christmas carol.

THE YEAR 1966 BEGAN WITH A PARTIAL VICTORY FOR THOSE WHO CALLED for negotiations to end the war. Bowing to pressure from critics, anticipating even more pressure when the bombing limits would soon be lifted, and hoping that there was a slight chance for bringing the Communists to the peace table, Johnson announced a bombing halt on December 25, 1965, and extended it through the end of January. When this action failed to bring about peace talks, after a flurry of activity during which time the president instructed his diplomats around the world to take a Communist diplomat to lunch, Johnson resumed the bombing. Fifteen senators and seventy-six representatives had urged the president to continue the pause indefinitely. Americans in general told pollsters they supported an end to the pause, but by the thinnest of margins, 44 to 42 percent. The administration would not accept the Communists' terms for starting negotiations, which included a complete and permanent cessation of the bombing without a reciprocal promise to stop infiltrating men and materiel into the south.

During the period of the bombing pause, three American activists, SDS cofounder Tom Hayden, Staughton Lynd, a radical history professor, and Herbert Aptheker, another historian and celebrated member of the CP, were in North Vietnam touring the country and engaging officials in political discussions about the war. They met with Premier Pham Van Dong, who, from their perspective, presented reasonable terms for peace, which Lynd shared with State Department officials on his return to the United States. Secretary of State Dean Rusk belittled such emissaries who always came home "eight months pregnant with peace."[3] Hayden and Lynd published a memoir of their trip, *The Other Side*, soon after they returned (Aptheker published a separate book), which painted a favorable picture of North Vietnam as a society directed by charming and reasonable leaders. Looking over the destruction wrought by the American bombs, Hayden remembered feeling the "fearlessness, calm determination, pride, even serenity," of the people of Hanoi.[4] Such trips were not necessarily in the best interests of the antiwar movement since most citizens were suspicious of any Americans who visited the enemy during "wartime."

EARLY IN JANUARY A CIVIL RIGHTS WORKER FROM SNCC WAS KILLED in Alabama. The organization asserted in response that the murder was "no different from the murder of people in Vietnam."[5] Although African Americans were rarely involved in early antiwar organizations and demonstrations, they too began more frequently to assail the United States government as the chief obstacle to peace and justice at home and abroad. While the administration had to worry about growing antiwar sentiment, it also had to be concerned about the growing radicalism among African-American civil rights advocates. The year 1966 was pivotal for that movement, with SNCC moving to the left, calling for Black Nationalism and not integration, and adopting Black Power as a slogan. Further, beginning with a riot in the Watts neighborhood of Los Angeles in the fall of 1965, a series of racial disturbances in over 100 cities over the next three years rocked the country, and many of those disturbances occurred in Northern cities that had not experienced legal segregation. Politicians and journalists conflated what they considered menacing marchers for Black Power with "riots" in the ghettoes and with perceived violence at antiwar demonstrations to cast aspersions on all protests during the period. No wonder most Americans not only refused to participate publicly in mass actions; they questioned the propriety, and even the right, of their fellow citizens to gather in large groups to oppose government policies.

FORTUNATELY FOR THE ANTIWAR MOVEMENT, FROM TIME TO TIME support came from respected figures airing their opposition in acceptable political formats. Such was the case in late January and early February 1966, when the chair of the Senate Foreign Relations Committee, Senator J. William Fulbright, turned a hearing on supplemental aid for South Vietnam into a nationally televised short course in the pros and cons of administration policy. Although that policy was ably defended by Dean Rusk among others, two moderate, adult, and anti-Communist experts took issue with it, as did several of the senators on the committee—in five televised sessions. General James Gavin, a much decorated and respected war hero, suggested that the military was not fighting the war in the proper way and offered an enclave strategy that would have slowed the pace of escalation. For his part, one of the originators of the containment policy, George Kennan, took issue with the underlying rationales for American involvement in Vietnam. Neither man advocated withdrawal but both offered harsh enough criticisms to legitimize for many Americans the adoption of antiwar positions. One of Johnson's aides expressed concern to him about the way the doves were using these misguided American patriots for their own purposes. The president himself ordered the FBI to investigate members of the Foreign Relations Committee who might have been influenced by their relationships with Communist diplomats.

The hearings were a major event for critics of the war. One of Tennessee senator Albert Gore's (senior) constituents wrote to him that she was so involved in the hearings that she had to tell her husband, "You have an unclean house but a highly informed wife."[6] But, as was the case throughout the era, antiwar activists relied on a wide variety of local events to promote their arguments.

Early in February, 100 war veterans traveled to Washington to turn in their medals and decorations. Later that month, prominent antiwar activist Jim Peck, who was able to obtain a ticket to a dinner in New York City where the president was to receive an award, jumped up in the middle of the ceremonies shouting, "Mr. President, Peace in Vietnam," a slogan he then displayed on the shirt under his jacket as he was led away. Outside, 4,000 pickets marched and chanted "Hey, Hey, LBJ, How Many Kids Did You Kill Today?" a couplet that was first heard at the SANE rally the previous November. It would beleaguer the president wherever he went in the United States—even in the White House when he opened the windows looking out on Pennsylvania Avenue. During the war, pickets were almost always parading in front of the White House, often in very small numbers, but their chants could be heard. They certainly could be heard during the wedding reception for Luci Johnson in August.

Never before in American history had presidents been subject to such rude behavior. It became impossible for Johnson and Nixon to travel to many venues to deliver speeches. And not all the jeerers were as decorous as Jim Peck. They often laced their interruptions with profanities that shocked the nation, at the end of an era when words like "bastard," "bitch," and worse were not seen in the newspapers, heard on the airwaves, or even spoken in Hollywood films. Now presidents heard not only the "Hey Hey" chant but "One, two, three, four, We don't want your fuckin war." No wonder Lady Bird Johnson's daily diary entries frequently included references to the absence or presence of picketers and other protesters whenever the First Family traveled outside the White House. The White House itself was not a haven. In January 1968, at a conference called by the First Lady to discuss juvenile delinquency, one of the invitees, entertainer Eartha Kitt, interrupted the proceedings to launch into a diatribe against the war.

Other antiwar actions during the first half of 1966 included a national campaign led by A. J. Muste and Joan Baez who, in April, joined with 3,000 of their supporters to refuse to pay taxes. Muste had not paid his taxes for nineteen years. Countless hundreds of thousands of other citizens during the war subtracted from their tax payment that amount they determined went to the Defense Department or specifically to support the war in Vietnam.

In May, an organization of American Writers and Artists Against the War in Vietnam including Lillian Hellman, John Hersey, Elmer Rice, and Alfred Kazin, held a series of "read-ins" to popularize their cause. Not since the 1930s, when the literary community rallied around the anti-Nazi banner, did so many novelists, essayists, and poets lend their names and talents to a cause. In fact, the previous June, when President Johnson sponsored a Festival of the Arts at the White House, several prominent invitees refused to attend because of the war, and several who did, including Hersey, disturbed the president by making the war the subject of their remarks. Johnson was not without his defenders. When the critic Dwight Macdonald asked actor Charlton Heston, a long-time Democratic liberal to sign an antiwar petition, Heston "ate his ass out" and told him what he could do with his petition.[7]

Also in May, SANE sponsored a National Voters Peace Pledge Campaign that produced 73,000 signatories who promised to vote for peace candidates in the congressional elections in the fall. At the organizational meeting for the campaign, activists broadened their agenda to include the calling of a National Conference for a New Politics, which ultimately led to an insurgency campaign in the contest for the Democratic presidential nomination in 1968.

Finally, in May 1966, a handful of housewives on the West Coast protested the use of napalm in Vietnam by temporarily blocking trucks delivering that deadly chemical for shipment to the war zone. (Napalm was a jellied gasoline, which, when ignited, produced horrible injuries and deaths among its human targets.) They also began a boycott of Saran Wrap since Dow, the company that made the napalm, also made the kitchen product. All of these actions contributed to the movement. Tom Wicker, then a reporter for the *New York Times* who had not yet made up his mind about the war, remembered that the napalm protesters "had a very profound impact on me" because they were "very ordinary women."[8]

On June 6 an antiwar advertisement signed by 6,400 educators and others appeared in the *New York Times*. The ad called for the cessation of military activities in Vietnam. It was not the first such ad nor would it be the last. On the surface, a bunch of college professors who did not represent the rest of the nation in terms of their politics and philosophies signing such an ad should have meant little to opinion monitors in the White House. Nonetheless, they clipped such advertisements, searched through them for important figures, and reported to their superiors about the relative eminence of the signatories. Someone in the White House was reading these petitions that usually appeared in the Sunday "News of the Week in Review" section.

The signers themselves had several motivations. Many of the advertisements requested donations to support upcoming demonstrations or to pay for other advertisements. In addition, academics, or other groups of people who lent their names to this type of activity, including actors and actresses, writers, nurses, social workers, and business people, hoped to attract others in their disciplines to support the antiwar cause announced in their public commitment. Further, this activity, which could cost an individual as little as $10, was a way to participate in the antiwar movement without having to attend a potentially unruly demonstration. Not all such ads made it into print. In 1966 the *Baltimore Sun* refused to run one that had been purchased by that city's Interfaith Peace Commission, most likely because its editors knew that the president read their paper.

In other actions in 1966 scores of students and faculty at Amherst College and New York University walked out of their graduation ceremonies in June in protest against the honorary degree awarded to former National Security Advisor McGeorge Bundy. As the war progressed, it became increasingly more difficult for colleges to present honorary degrees to anyone associated with the administration. At commencements such as those at Yale and the University of California in 1968 and 1969, scores of graduates made public pledges to resist the draft and induction. In 1970, Richard Nixon was angered to discover that he could not attend his own daughter Julie's graduation at Smith College because of the disruption he would cause by appearing in Northhampton, Massachusetts. On June 20, 1966, the Internal Security Subcommittee of the Senate Judiciary Committee claimed that Communists were manipulating campus grievances for their own political purposes, a charge that was, if not untrue, certainly wildly exaggerated.

Finally, 1966 marked the escalation of draft and draft-related protests that began when David J. Miller burned his draft card in New York City the previous October. In the first of several raids, Barry Bondhus broke into the draft board in Big Lake, Minnesota and destroyed hundreds of records of men with a 1A classification by pouring human feces on them.

Far more threatening to the military system was the case of the Fort Hood Three. In late June, three soldiers, a White, an African American and a Hispanic American, refused to go to Vietnam because "we will not be part of this unjust, immoral war [with its] criminal waste of American lives."[9] They contended, as did other draft resisters and deserters, that the war was illegal and immoral for two reasons: Congress had not declared it and it was fought using immoral means. By accepting orders to fight in Vietnam, they would be violating the Nuremberg precedent that emerged from the trials of Nazis after World War II. There the prosecution argued that soldiers must disobey orders, which though legal in their country, violated Judeo-Christian principles. Throughout the Vietnam era, no judge accepted those arguments as they maintained the issues raised were political and not justiciable. The Fort Hood Three were court-martialed and received two years in prison. They did appeal to the U.S. Supreme Court but liberal justice William O. Douglas was the only one willing to listen to their arguments.

Such arguments also failed to free Howard Levy, an army doctor, who, in October, refused to train Green Berets going to Vietnam. In his 1967 trial, despite the support of witnesses such as Benjamin Spock, world famous nutritionist Dr. Jean Mayer, and Robin Moore, an expert on the Green Berets, Levy was sentenced to three years at hard labor. The Fort Hood Three and Levy, who inspired others to take comparable actions in the years to come, became sources of encouragement to their comrades in the antiwar movement.

All of this local activism was useful to the movement in 1966, which was not a major year for dramatic mass demonstrations. The NCCEWVN did promote its Second International Days of Protest on the weekend of March 25-27. But the seemingly impressive attendance—100,000 participants in 80 cities with 20,000 or more in New York City—was not much larger than that of the First International Days of Protest the previous October. And again, at least in the media, radicals and those who practiced civil and uncivil disobedience dominated these events. *Newsweek* was not alone with its story lead, "As U.S. troops score a succession of fresh victories in Vietnam, peace groups in the U.S. doggedly cranked up" with demonstrations full of "strident marchers."[10] Few reports noted that several African Americans appeared at the New York rally carrying signs that read, "The Vietcong Never Called Me a Nigger," a slogan that would later be appropriated by the draft-resisting heavyweight boxing champion, Muhammad Ali, and still later, with a variation, "The Vietcong Never Called me a Chick," by women's liberation groups.

The lack of positive public and media response to the March protests helped to dampen interest in a fall protest. The year 1966 was the only one from 1965 through 1971 that did not feature at least one nationwide demonstration in the spring and another in the fall. But the movement was percolating from below in a variety of different ways, including planning for mass demonstrations in 1967. At a Cleveland conference in July, sociology professor Sidney Peck and other activists called for another meeting in late November that would establish a new nationwide coalition to organize national demonstrations. Out of that meeting, whose leadership included Peck, Muste, and Dellinger, the Spring Mobilization Committee to End the War in Vietnam was established. This organization evolved after the spring 1967 events into a National Mobilization Committee and later the New Mobilization Committee. The Spring Mobe was the first somewhat centrally organized antiwar coalition, but it was still a loose confederation featuring a good deal of regional autonomy. Non exclusionary, its national and regional officers included representatives from most of the leftwing political and pacifist groups. However, the leadership of an offshoot, the Student Mobe, was ultimately taken over by the YSA, the SWP's creation.

At the Cleveland meeting, several key issues arose that would affect the movement's organizational difficulties throughout the era. When the parties and sects on the left adopted a non-exclusionary approach, they guaranteed constant infighting and struggling for power among groups that harbored historic hostility toward one another. Those groups clung to strong and conflicting ideas about whether they should concentrate exclusively on the war or try to develop into a multi-issue movement. In addition, left-sectarian groups like the SWP, which did not have much of a nationwide grassroots base, depended upon their cadres in several large cities. Thus, they tended to support national demonstrations rather than local and decentralized actions.

One reason for the failure of the antiwarriors to take to the streets of Washington or New York in the fall was the decision, opposed by SDS and SWP, to work on the congressional campaigns in the summer and fall of 1966 in order to bring more doves to Capitol Hill. The SDS and SWP did not think congressional work was an unworthy idea in and of itself; they merely thought the movement should use its limited energies and resources elsewhere, in more mass actions or in draft resistance. SWP also had a long-standing theoretical opposition to working with capitalist political parties. Here we can see a curious parallel between the movement's options at home and the U.S. military's options in Vietnam. There the choice was between emphasizing defense and something like General Gavin's enclave approach or taking the war to the enemy with the administration's search-and-destroy attrition strategy being implemented by General William Westmoreland. No one who supported Westmoreland thought that Gavin's approach was intrinsically unworkable; it was simply not as good as theirs, and the army did not have the resources to do both well at the same time.

During the congressional campaigns, peace groups supported two dozen candidates, all of whom lost. The most important election took place in the liberal Bay Area of northern California where Robert Scheer, a radical journalist associated with the slick leftist journal, *Ramparts,* ran against Jeffrey Cohelan, a liberal Democrat who supported the war. Although Scheer lost, he received 45 percent of the vote. For a while, former Berkeley graduate student Jerry Rubin, who later became a counter-cultural leader and prankster in the Yippie Party, served as Scheer's campaign manager. The White House carefully observed the contest and did all that it could to support Cohelan.

In some ways the 1966 war referendum in Dearborn, Michigan, was more troubling for the president. During the war, many municipalities, which obviously had no direct role in the making of foreign policy, sponsored referendums on the war to demonstrate their concerns to Washington. Dearborn was a blue-collar suburb of Detroit, whose mayor, Orville Hubbard, was a famous anti-integrationist with a slogan, "Hubbard keeps Dearborn clean," which meant all white. But Hubbard was an ex-marine who was convinced that the war in Vietnam was not the best way to spend American military resources. He was also concerned about the unfairness of the draft, which saw many more of his constituents ending up in Vietnam than those from more affluent suburbs. Forty-one percent of those who voted in Dearborn agreed with the language of the referendum that called for an immediate cease-fire and the withdrawal of American troops. Hubbard himself was something of an embarrassment to the peace movement, because of his perceived racism. When he showed up at an antiwar rally at Detroit's Cobo Hall in 1967 and demanded his right as an elected official to sit on the dais, organizers reluctantly had to give him a seat with the others, albeit far from the center of the action.

The 1966 campaigns encouraged two insurgent Democrats, Curtis Gans and Allard Lowenstein, to challenge Johnson in the 1968 primaries if the war continued. Although the attempt to elect peace candidates had failed, the once omnipotent president's political power was beginning to weaken as the Scheer candidacy and the Dearborn referendum demonstrated. Moreover, the election of Ronald Reagan to the governorship in California, and Republican gains in Congress, in part a response to the perceived radicalism of Democrats, augured ill for Johnson's ability to lead. A Reagan aide boasted, "We jumped on [student unrest] as an issue." A former Democrat and union leader, Reagan scored points during the period by deriding the peace slogan, "Make Love, Not War"—"The only trouble was they didn't look like they were capable of doing either. Their hair was cut like Tarzan, and they acted like Jane, and they smelled like Cheetah."[11]

Antiwar activity in democratic societies was worldwide. When Johnson visited Australia and New Zealand in October, 1966, he was confronted by chanting picketers virtually everywhere he went. One could argue that this constant harassment, whether outside the White House or 8,000 miles away, could make a stubborn man even more stubborn. He was the first president in modern history to be subjected to such constant public disrespect. It demeaned him personally as well as the office he held. Although he may have understood, as he often said, why the scruffy, foul-mouthed chanters were so critical of his policies in Vietnam, they still angered him and may have made him even less likely to change course. He was so averse to confronting them that he ordered his aides to shorten the lead time between the announcement of a trip and the trip itself in order to foil demonstration organizers. Yet they still managed to show up. That fact, and that he encountered picketers wherever he went shouting the same slogans and carrying the same placards, helped convince him that they were part of a worldwide conspiracy orchestrated by Moscow and its allies— another reason to ignore their arguments.

He might try to ignore the movement but other members of his administration could not. They too were picketed wherever they went—often in front of their homes in Washington and the outlying districts. On one celebrated occasion in early November, 1966, Secretary of Defense McNamara came close to suffering serious bodily injury at the hands of a mob, in of all places, Harvard Square. McNamara had agreed to talk to selected Harvard students in a private session. When word leaked out, other students and young people in the area, organized by SDS leaders, discovered his whereabouts and surrounded and rocked his car, demanding that he emerge to engage them in an educational give and take. He was forced to do so, answered a few questions in a surly confrontation, and then beat a hasty retreat. To be challenged at the seat of the American establishment by irreverent and impolite students was quite shocking for McNamara. (Vice President Hubert Humphrey faced almost as dangerous a situation after an appearance at Stanford University in February 1967.)

Unbeknownst to the students, and indeed to most of his colleagues in the administration, by the middle of 1966, McNamara had become convinced that the bombing was not working and that the United States had to figure out a way to withdraw from Vietnam in an honorable manner. It pained him that many doves, knowing of his support for the bombing of North Vietnam, had begun talking about "McNamara's War." His wife and three children had made known their dovish inclinations, as had scores of his political friends, including intimates from the Kennedy camp. An emotionally fragile man, the confrontation in Cambridge further rattled him.

McNamara was not the only one rattled by the front page of the *New York Times* on Christmas morning, 1966. In the first of a series of sensational articles that would appear in the most important newspaper in the world over the next few weeks, Harrison Salisbury, one of the *Times's* most distinguished columnists, described how Hanoi and the surrounding area had been devastated by U.S. bombing. Up to this point, whenever antiwar critics talked about the murder of civilians by American bombardiers, the administration insisted it was hitting only military targets in the most surgical bombing in history. It dismissed claims about damage to civilian targets as propaganda.

Salisbury reported that many civilians had been killed and wounded and that American bombs had destroyed schools, hospitals, and residential sections. To be sure, Salisbury was led into exaggerating the damage by his hosts, but the United States could no longer insist that civilians were not dying in its air war against North Vietnam. Salisbury himself was assailed by many other journalists and politicians as a traitor. Nonetheless, the new line emanating from the Defense Department accepted the general plausibility of Salisbury's stories but insisted that its flyers did not deliberately target civilians and their homes and structures; civilians were hit in error and because they were located near military targets that had been cruelly placed by the Communists in civilian areas. Such admissions demonstrated that the antiwar movement, which had made the bombing of North Vietnam one of the centerpieces of its charge that the United States was fighting an immoral war, had been right all along. As the initial bombing in February 1965 had served as a catalyst for the antiwar movement, the Salisbury reports served to reinvigorate it, with, for example, one Harvard philosophy professor quickly gathering 6,000 signatures from faculty who opposed bombing North Vietnam from 200 colleges in 37 states. The reports also demonstrated once again the symbiotic relationships among the media, the antiwar movement, and public opinion.

The apparent immorality of the war symbolized by the bombing contributed significantly to the growth of antiwar sentiment among American religious leaders. The year 1966 marked the foundation of their most important group, the Clergy and Laymen Concerned About Vietnam (CALCAV). There were always peace churches in the United States and, even more important, all the major religions believed in fairly strict moral and political guidelines before they would support their nation's participation in a "just war." To many, the war in Vietnam was not a just war.

As early as September 15, 1963, after Buddhist self-immolations, the Ministers' Vietnam Committee took an ad in the *New York Times* opposing Washington's support for the Saigon regime, and the use of "immoral" tactics in the war. The twelve clerics who signed the ad, including the distinguished theologians Reinhold Niebuhr and Harry Emerson Fosdick, claimed they were speaking for 17,000 other clergy and citizens. In April 1965, the Clergymen's Emergency Committee For Vietnam took an ad in the *Times* signed by 2,500 religious leaders who opposed the bombing of North Vietnam. In May, an Interreligious Committee on Vietnam, whose leaders included John C. Bennett, the President of the Union Theological Seminary and Martin Luther King, Jr., promoted a silent vigil at the Pentagon. King, who was concerned about alienating an administration that had been so favorable to the cause of civil rights, was not yet in the forefront of clerical critics of the war. The next month, a delegation of American clergy traveled to South Vietnam to see what could be done to bring about a negotiated end to the war. By the fall of 1965, the National Council of Churches, the Catholic Peace Fellowship, the Union of Hebrew Congregations, and the Protestant journal *Christianity and Crisis* had all expressed severe reservations about the U.S. involvement in Southeast Asia. Summing up many of their feelings, Niebuhr, who previously had endorsed the American approach to the Cold War, announced, "For the first time I fear I am ashamed of our beloved nation."[12]

Thus it was on October 25, 1965, that one hundred clergy met in New York to organize a permanent antiwar organization. The ecumenical group of leaders at this session included Rabbi Abraham Heschel, a renowned professor at the Jewish Theological Seminary, Reverend Richard Neuhaus of the Lutheran church, St. John the Evangelist, and a Jesuit priest, Daniel Berrigan. On January 11, 1966, these leaders and others announced the formation of the National Emergency Committee of Clergy Concerned About Vietnam, which became CALCAV. By the end of the year, CALCAV claimed sixty-eight chapters; by the middle of 1967 it added ten more and boasted a membership mailing list of 12,000. Those numbers grew to 100 locals and a mailing list of 25,000 by 1969.

CALCAV began as a relatively moderate antiwar organization, calling in 1966 for a negotiated peace and an end to escalation. It advocated such positions through petitions, vigils, ads, and, at the start, opposed civil disobedience. In 1967 alone, CALCAV mailed out over 1.4 million pieces of literature. Like other coalitions, this one had difficulty maintaining unity, particularly as some members of the clergy wanted to move beyond approved tactics to civil disobedience. Moreover, after Israel won the Middle East war of 1967 and then occupied Arab territories, some leftists in the clergy and elsewhere began attacking the Jewish state as an imperialist power. These attacks led to a decline in Jewish-American support for CALCAV, and for the increasingly radical antiwar movement in general.

Moreover, the Catholic Church hierarchy was not as outspoken about the war, despite Pope Paul VI's criticisms, as were Protestant leaders. In January 1967, the nation's most famous Catholic prelate, Francis Cardinal Spellman, labeled the war "Christ's war," a statement that led to a protest at his church, New York's St. Patrick's Cathedral, in which demonstrators carried signs reading, "Thou shall not kill in Vietnam." CALCAV enjoyed only minority support in the Protestant community as well. Throughout the period, the majority of America's Protestant clergy did not participate in its activities. Indeed, even for those who did, a good portion of their congregations did not necessarily follow them into the antiwar camp.

All the same, the energetic participation in antiwar activities of scores of the most prominent religious leaders contributed dramatically to the success of the movement. Their presence at rallies and marches legitimized protest for many middle-class adult Americans and their frequent discussion of Vietnam in their weekly sermons promoted dovish sentiments among their congregations. And they influenced other leaders as well. Minnesota senator Eugene McCarthy, who within a year would challenge Lyndon Johnson for the presidential nomination, delivered his first major public speech on the war on February 1, 1967, after having been lobbied in Washington by members of CALCAV the previous day.

OF ALL THE YEARS FROM 1965 THROUGH 1971, 1966 APPEARED ON the surface to be the least important in terms of the impact of the antiwar movement on policy and opinion. It certainly is true that the movement made more headlines during other years. Yet during 1966, activists continued to mobilize in ever greater numbers, testing tactics and forming organizations that would soon attract considerable attention, especially as Vietnam continued to swallow up more and more of the nation's human and financial resources.

NOTES

1. Anderson, *The Movement*, 151.

2. DeBenedetti, *An American Ordeal*, 156–57.

3. Small, *Johnson, Nixon, and the Doves*, 88.

4. Tom Hayden, *Reunion: A Memoir* (New York: Random House, 1988), 183.

5. Zaroulis and Sullivan, *Who Spoke Up?* 69.

6. Small, *Johnson, Nixon, and the Doves*, 79.

7. Ibid., 52.

8. Wells, *The War Within*, 86.

9. Zaroulis and Sullivan, *Who Spoke Up?* 87.

10. Small, *Covering Dissent*, 63.

11. Gerald J. DeGroot, *A Noble Cause: America and the Vietnam War* (New York: Pearson, 2000), 321, 322.

12. Hall, *Because of Their Faith*, 30.

CHAPTER Four

BECOMING A MASS MOVEMENT

LTHOUGH LYNDON JOHNSON APPEARED TO BE IN NO IMMINENT political danger because of his Vietnam policies in 1966, his fortunes declined rapidly in 1967. In the fall of 1964 and again in the summer of 1965, Undersecretary of State George Ball, one of the few who counseled against escalation, had warned that the war of attrition in Vietnam would be a long one and that the longer it continued, the more Americans would become disenchanted with the venture. He pointed to the Korean War, when after a year or so of limited war, the public began to lose its patience. And that was a war in which few Americans opposed the intervention.

As 1967 began, 32 percent of those polled thought that intervention had been a mistake. By the end of the year that number rose to 45 percent. However, only 10 percent of Americans demanded an immediate withdrawal, with many of those who thought intervention a mistake advocating hawkish military policies in which their country would unleash all of its might to produce a speedy victory. Of great concern were the doubling of the yearly battle-death totals from 5,000 in 1966 to 10,000 in 1967 and the increase of troops in the combat theater from 385,000 to almost 500,000 by year's end. Throughout 1967, as the movement continued to promote a wide variety of imaginative national and local activities, increasing numbers of politicians, journalists, and other public figures began to express their opposition to American intervention.

LEADERS OF THE MOVEMENT WERE CONSTANTLY CONCERNED ABOUT the need to adopt new, attention-getting tactics—in the words of David Dellinger, "to keep moving forward."[1] The February 13, 1967 petition to the White House from 5,000 scientists calling for a study of chemical and biological warfare and antipersonnel weapons and the sit-in that same day in the area where Dow Chemical, a maker of body bags and napalm, was recruiting University of Wisconsin students attracted a good deal of attention. Anti-Dow protests at Wisconsin, long a hotbed of activism, continued through the year with sixty people injured in a violent clash between students and the police in October. The police overreaction on that occasion resulted in student and faculty boycotts of classes and the university's chancellor posting bail for those arrested. At the same time one state assemblyman excoriated the "long haired, greasy pigs" and another exclaimed, "Shoot them if necessary. I would. It's insurrection."[2]

Another Mother for Peace, which launched its antiwar program in March in Beverly Hills, California, attracted even more attention. Its co-chair was the actress Donna Reed who was known to virtually all Americans through her celebrated television role as a wholesome, almost-too-good-to-be-true, apolitical housewife. The organization's slogan, soon seen on Mother's Day cards and bumper stickers, was the compelling "War is not healthy for children and other living things." It became even more famous than WSP's "Not our Sons, Not Your Sons, Not Their Sons," which appeared on banners at a Washington protest in February. By 1968, Another Mother for Peace had 100,000 members; three years later, it claimed 240,000 subscribers to its newsletter, almost all of them middle-class women and mothers who, in many ways, posed a more serious political threat to the White House than 200,000 demonstrating college students and young people who had never voted and who did not belong to political parties.

It is true, however, that by 1967, some antiwar women activists had begun to concentrate on their own issues, in part because of their experiences in the movement. One slogan encouraging draft resistance, which some antiwar women employed on their placards and posters was indicative: "Girls Say Yes to Men Who Say No." Many women were offended by the sexist nature of the quid pro quo. In January 1968, WSP organized the Jeannette Rankin Brigade's demonstration in Washington. Rankin, the Montana pacifist who was the first women elected to Congress in 1916 and who was reelected in 1940, voted against U.S. entry into the two world wars. Some of the 5,000 brigade members broke off from their colleagues to march to Arlington National Cemetery for a symbolic burial of traditional womanhood. However, not all members of such organizations as WILPF and WSP were ardent feminists. As WSP leader Cora Weiss commented, "We were all young women with children and families" who were engaged in marching and lobbying sometimes "without their husband's full approval."[3]

Some women devoted themselves to both the women's and the peace movements but most activists chose to concentrate their energies on one or another. Nina Adams, who began working in the antiwar movement while a college student, was typical of those who concentrated on the war. "The Vietnam War," she explained, "occupied twelve years of my life, dominated my politics, delayed my dissertation, took me past my confused career goals into understanding where my commitments are."[4] Nonetheless, feminist issues colored the way she and other women looked at the war. For example, some of them made common cause with the women of the Vietcong and North Vietnam who, it appeared, were more liberated than American women, at least in terms of their apparent leadership roles in all aspects of society, including the diplomatic corps and the government. As one revolutionary woman, a Black Panther, explained, "The Vietnamese women are out there fighting with their brothers, fighting against American imperialism. . . . They can shoot. They're out there with their babies on their backs."[5]

DESPITE DEFECTIONS TO THE WOMEN'S LIBERATION ORGANIZATIONS, women, particularly housewives, were among the most important participants in the antiwar movement. The same could not be said for African Americans. Only a small minority of them had made common cause with the people of color against whom their country was waging war in Asia. Until 1967, most African-American leaders had not involved themselves with the antiwar movement. Moderates did not want to attack the president who had done so much for civil rights. Radicals who advocated Black Power, black nationalism, and even separatism opposed the war but did not generally cooperate with the leadership of the antiwar movement. The Black Panther platform did proclaim, "We will not fight and kill other people in the world, who, like black people, are being victimized by the white racist government in America."[6] In 1967 several of the more radical antiwar leaders met in secret with H. Rap Brown, a SNCC official who was then a fugitive from justice, but failed to convince him to work with their coalitions.

Into this milieu in the spring of 1967 the most prominent black leader, Martin Luther King, Jr., threw himself wholeheartedly into the antiwar movement. King, while increasingly popular among White Americans because of his relative moderation compared to the Black nationalists, had begun to lose support within the African-American community, especially among young people. Although it had denounced the war, SNCC had also denounced cooperating with White radicals in 1966. Moreover, in July of that year, CORE, another group that eschewed cooperation with the antiwar movement, had called for the immediate withdrawal of American forces from Vietnam. Aside from the growing strength of African-American groups to his left, King considered it his duty as a Nobel Peace Prize winner, who had privately anguished over the war, to speak out in forceful terms against its continuation. In addition, he had moved to the left in recent months, more and more seeing the centrality of reforming the economic system to any program that would ameliorate the plight of poor Americans. A government study revealed a 35 percent decline in funding for social programs in fiscal 1968, a decline that could be traced to the rising costs of the Vietnam War. Finally, a *Ramparts* magazine expose about the use of napalm in Vietnam had troubled King deeply.

Thus it was in a Chicago address on March 25, 1967, that he asserted, "We are committing atrocities equal to any perpetrated by the Vietcong" and the bombing in Vietnam may well "destroy the dream and possibility for a decent America."[7] King drew even more attention with his sensational remarks at the Riverside Memorial Church in New York City ten days later, when he made the connection between the war in Vietnam and the struggle for civil rights in the United States—"We were taking the black young men ... and sending them eight thousand miles away to guarantee liberties in Southeast

Asia which they had not found in Southwest Georgia or East Harlem."
In his most quoted sentence from the speech, he labeled the United States
"the greatest purveyor of violence in the world today."[8] For such inflammatory remarks, King was denounced by baseball hero Jackie Robin-
son in the *Amsterdam News* and by the head of the NAACP. Presidential aide John Roche told his boss, that King "has thrown in with the
commies," and that he was "inordinately ambitious and quite stupid."[9]

With his Riverside Church speech, King became an instant leader
of the antiwar movement. King's defection from the administration was
the second such political body blow dealt the Johnson administration
in 1967. In February, New York's Democratic senator Robert F.
Kennedy had broken with the president over Vietnam policy. Almost
immediately, activists, who were already pushing Kennedy to challenge
Johnson in the primaries, talked about running King for president on
a third-party ticket, and the administration feared he might attract as
many as one-third to one-half of the traditionally Democratic Black
voters.

In whatever movement African-American leaders decided to place
their energies, they had little control over the 218 urban disturbances
that took place in 1967. Twenty-one people died in the riots in Newark
and forty-three in Detroit in a disturbance or insurrection that also
resulted in $85 million in property damages and the need to call out
4,700 paratroopers of the 101st Airborne Division. In the wake of the
disturbances, a federal commission asked rioters and non-rioters in the
two cities if they thought that their country was worth fighting for. In
Detroit, 39 percent said no, compared to 15 percent of non-rioters; in
Newark the comparable figures were 53 and 28 percent, respectively.

By 1968, serious racial conflict had spread to the military services,
greatly concerning the admirals and generals who had to deal with
unprecedented riots, fights, and insubordination from their men in the
combat theater. Stateside, in 1969, Joe Miles, a Black Trotskyist, established the GI's United Against the War at Fort Jackson, North Carolina; while abroad, an estimated 1,000 Blacks formed the African-
American Draft Resisters group in Canada, claiming they were refugees
from slavery. At least fourteen of the eighty military deserters in Sweden in mid-1968 were African Americans. During that same period,
Americans expressed shock when Tommie Smith and John Carlos, two
of the medalists in the 200 meters race at the Mexico City Olympics,

raised their black-gloved hands in a Black Power salute on the winners' platform while the "Star Spangled Banner" was being played.
Two years later, in a celebrated comment on the indictment of Black
Panther leader Bobby Seale for murder, the president of Yale University, Kingman Brewster, said he was "skeptical about the ability of
black revolutionaries to achieve a fair trial in the United States."[10]
Many young Blacks agreed with SNCC leader Stokely Carmichael who
had complained in 1967 about "white people sending black people to
make war on yellow people in order to defend the land they stole from
red people."[11]

RAMPARTS MAGAZINE, A MUCKRAKING LEFT-WING MONTHLY, WAS
another important ally in the movement. In March 1967 it broke a
story about the secret CIA funding of the National Student Association. Earlier, in an issue that featured Madame Nhu on the cover in a
Michigan State University cheerleader's outfit, *Ramparts* revealed sensational information about the university's involvement in training the
brutal South Vietnamese secret police. At the next major antiwar
demonstration in New York, quite a few marchers carried placards
that read, "End University Complicity," a slogan that encompassed
classified research for the military, recruiting on campus for government work or for such blacklisted firms as Dow Chemical, and cooperating with the Selective Service System.

   Ramparts was not the only source for radical perspectives on the
issues of the day. The period 1965–1973 was the heyday of the independent weekly newspaper. Often relying on the same left-wing
national news services, the *Berkeley Barb,* the *Free Press* in Los Angeles, the *East Village Other* in New York, and the *Fifth Estate* in Detroit,
among many others, joined the older *Village Voice* and the *Guardian*
to offer detailed news about the war, the movement, and other political and cultural activities of the era that were not always covered in
the mainstream press. In addition, appealing to a more adult and intel-
lectually oriented clientele, the *New York Review of Books,* founded
in 1963 during a newspaper strike, was a major source for lengthy and
cerebral articles about the war and the "revolution."

   The Spring Mobilization in New York City on April 15, 1967 was
the largest and most impressive antiwar demonstration to date. At least
250,000, and perhaps more, marched in the rain in New York City

from Central Park to the United Nations where keynoter Martin Luther King, Jr., delivered a petition to Ralph Bunche, the undersecretary of the world body and fellow Nobel Peace Prize laureate. In addition to King, the marchers listened to songs from Harry Belafonte and Pete Seeger, and to speeches from Nobel Prize winning scientist Linus Pauling, Norman Mailer, television's "Man from UNCLE" Robert Vaughn, Benjamin Spock, and SNCC's Stokely Carmichael. The participation of Carmichael reflected the Mobe's attempt to attract as broad an audience as possible. One member of WSP who was present remarked that she was "constantly astonished, yet again, at the disparate elements that a peace demonstration can encompass."[12]

SANE, among the more moderate of the groups involved, was not so astonished. Concerned about the dominance of radical groups in the leadership of the Mobe, it decided against a national endorsement of the march, permitting instead its locals to decide their own positions. Many liberals were not pleased when Carmichael called the president a "buffoon" and a "fool" in comments that received more attention from the media than those of King.

On the eve of the march, the House Committee on Un-American Activities (HUAC) had issued a report describing the Mobe as being dominated by Communists who had duped liberals and pacifists. Moreover, as it was to do in other antiwar activities, the FBI, which did not need HUAC's report to inform it about the movement, waved the red flag to its sources in the media. Such overt and covert preemptive strikes from government officials before large demonstrations were quite common through both the Johnson and Nixon administrations. Further, Johnson, and later Richard Nixon, believed that international communism was behind much of the American antiwar movement. They encouraged the FBI, the CIA, the NSA, and other security agencies to observe carefully and harass antiwar groups, often violating the Constitution as they did so. In 1975, after a series of hearings concerning these and other flagrant violations of civil liberties in which the absence of evidence of communist infiltration of the New Left and civil rights and antiwar movements became clear, Congress enacted laws to restrain U.S. intelligence agencies.

In addition to endorsing tacitly the attempt to weaken if not destroy such organizations through the use of agents provocateurs, unnecessary tax audits, and other illegal acts, both Johnson and Nixon on several occasions commissioned the CIA to uncover the formal links between Moscow and her allies and the peace movement. Although the agency could demonstrate that antiwar leaders corresponded with and met foreign Communists, it disappointed both presidents when it could turn up no smoking guns relating to foreign financing or policy direction from the Cominform.

Whether or not "Communists" were prominent among the leadership of the Mobe, there is no doubt that members of the Trotskyist SWP enjoyed considerable influence in planning strategy and tactics. The vast majority of those who marched under the Mobe banner were unaware, or did not care, that radicals were the chief organizers of the event. They had to be annoyed, however, by those who marched among them carrying Ho Chi Minh and Che Guevara posters and endlessly repeating obscene slogans and chants.

On the other hand, the political radicals in charge of the Spring Mobilization were not that radical, at least when it came to civil disobedience. They often crossed swords with radical pacifists who constantly called for employing the tactic they had used in scores of other demonstrations for several generations. Originally, a group of young men planned to come forward at the United Nations to burn their draft cards on the speakers' platform. Mobe leaders, pushed by SANE, WSP, and CALCAV, decided to separate the mass draft-card burning from the rally at the UN. Thus it was at Central Park's Sheep Meadow, some distance from the marchers, that more than 100 demonstrators gathered to burn their cards. Among them was Gary Rader, a former Green Beret. The previous spring, Rader had begun to turn against the war after reading a celebrated expose in *Ramparts* by another Green Beret, Donald Duncan.

Other former and current military personnel from Veterans for Peace participated in the march, with one, Jan Barry, carrying a banner that read, "Vietnam Veterans Against the War." It was out of this activity that Barry, a veteran and West Point dropout and five of his friends organized the Vietnam Veterans Against the War (VVAW) on June 1. Its emblem was an upturned rifle with a helmet on its butt end—the emblem of the American army in Vietnam was an upturned sword. Several months later, the VVAW set up LINK, the Serviceman's Link to the Peace Movement, to work directly with active-duty dissidents. During the Nixon administration, especially, the VVAW would play an important role in the movement.

Draft resistance was also a centerpiece of the sister demonstration in equally rainy San Francisco, where African-American leaders Julian

Bond and Coretta Scott King were among those who addressed the crowd. The Georgia State Legislature had denied Bond the seat to which he had been elected in November because of his antiwar statements. After his constituents elected him two more times in 1966, the Supreme Court ruled in November that the legislature had deprived him of his rights and that he had to be seated.

The over 50,000 people who jammed Kezar Stadium on April 15, 1967 heard a call for a national "turn-in" of draft cards on October 16. This meeting marked the first major appearance of The Resistance, a new antiwar group from the Palo Alto (California) Commune, which focused on the Selective Service System. Its main spokesperson was David Harris, president of Stanford's student body, who explained:

> The Resistance is a group of men who are bound together by one single and clear commitment: on October 16 we will hand in our draft cards and refuse any further cooperation with the Selective Service System. By doing so, we will actively challenge the government's right to draft American men for its criminal war against the people of Vietnam.[13]

Harris, who later married Joan Baez, served twenty months in prison for his own draft resistance. Of his sentence, he noted, "I find no more honorable position in modern America than that of a criminal."[14] Imprisoned Teamster union leader James Hoffa, who met another jailed draft resister at his penitentiary, allegedly railed, "You pacifists, whaddya know about organizing and picket lines. You're never going to get anywhere. You need fists and guns."[15]

By the time of Harris's announcement at Kezar Stadium, there were at least two dozen "We Won't Go" organizations on college campuses. Moreover, the AFSC, WSP, and others had established draft-counseling centers on and off campus to help young men legally, and sometimes illegally, escape the draft. During a five-month period in 1966–67, a *Handbook for Conscientious Objectors* sold 11,000 copies in five months. Another best-seller of the era was a pamphlet titled, "How to Lower Your Blood Pressure," while other pamphlets explained how to feign homosexuality, bedwetting, and drug addiction.

During the Vietnam era, over 170,000 young men were granted conscientious objector (CO) status while over 300,000 applications were denied. The courts became increasingly lenient over the period by broadening the definition to include not only religious beliefs but also moral beliefs. The courts also permitted successful appeals on occasion from those who opposed the Vietnam War and other "immoral" wars but not necessarily all wars. The new definitions were not much help to the 17,000 enlisted men who also tried to obtain CO status. By the late '60s, one-tenth of all federal court cases involved draft issues. One of the strategies of the draft-resistance movement was to flood the courts and the prisons with so many cases that the system would break down.

When in March 1967, a National Commission on Draft Reform recommended abolishing student deferments because they were unfair to those not in college, an administration aide thought that if that recommendation were accepted, as many as 25 percent of college students would refuse either to register or to heed their draft call. In June, the draft law was extended with undergraduate deferments intact but graduate-student deferments were all but eliminated for most of the social sciences and humanities. From 1965 through 1967, graduate schools had enjoyed an enrollment boom, in part from graduating seniors who wanted to extend their student deferments. After 1967, graduate programs exempted from the new rule, such as divinity schools, enjoyed an even greater enrollment boom. Student deferments were the reason that as many as 80 percent of the men who served in Vietnam came from working-class backgrounds. Only 17 percent of college students came from that socioeconomic class.

In April 1967, heavyweight boxing champion Muhammed Ali became the most famous person to refuse induction, arguing among other things, that he was exempted because he was a minister in the Nation of Islam and a religious conscientious objector. Ali asked rhetorically, "Who is this white man . . . to order a descendant of slaves to fight other people in their own country?"[16] Many Americans had been angered when Cassius Clay became a Black nationalist leader named Muhammed Ali. The patriotic National Boxing Association stripped him of his title and refused to sanction his bouts in the United States, while his case made its way on appeal to the Supreme Court. In June 1971, in an 8–0 decision, the court ruled in his favor. Almost as important in 1967 was the indictment of Carl Wilson, the lead singer of the Beach Boys, the quintessential West Coast surfing rock band, for failing to report for alternate service.

THE ANTIWAR MOVEMENT WAS THRILLED BY THE IMMENSE TURNOUT for the Spring Mobilization. It reinvigorated many foot soldiers who returned to their communities to work on grassroots campaigns and to prepare for the next big events in the fall. They could not have been pleased, however, with the less than favorable treatment they received in the mainstream media. *Time* felt the New York protest was "about as damaging as a blow from daffodils" for the administration although it must have been "delighting [for] Ho Chi Minh."[17] Such coverage frustrated those who participated in the march, the largest antiwar demonstration in American history, which aside from the separate draft-card burning, was peaceful and decorous. But not decorous enough, as the television cameras focused on the most outrageous "performers" in the antiwar van. As had been the case with previous demonstrations, letters to the White House favoring the administration's Vietnam policy increased for a few weeks after the Spring Mobilization before falling to previous levels. Many Americans apparently did not like the typical demonstrator they saw on television or in the stories in the newspapers. How could they know that, in fact, those demonstrators were atypical?

Despite the way the media framed their stories, by the spring of 1967, the administration was beginning to feel pressure from the movement. On April 24, for example, just nine days after the massive New York demonstration, influential liberals announced the formation of Negotiations Now! Among those endorsing the call for a bombing halt, cease fire and negotiations, but not for an immediate withdrawal, were a liberal all-star team that included Victor Reuther of the United Automobile Workers, economist and diplomat John Kenneth Galbraith, former Kennedy and Johnson aide Arthur Schlesinger, Jr., Democratic strategist Joseph Rauh, Norman Cousins of SANE, Martin Luther King, Jr., and business leader Marriner J. Eccles. In May, Eccles and 300 executives sent Johnson a letter, which was published in the *New York Times, Washington Post,* and the *Wall Street Journal,* supporting Negotiations Now!'s program. By September, 300 more businesspeople had signed on. That month, other business leaders had formed a permanent organization, Business Executives Move for Vietnam Peace (BEM), which began with over 1,600 members. BEM contended, "As businessmen we feel that when a policy hasn't proven productive after a reasonable trial it's sheer nonsense not to try to change it."[18] Some in the business community were not only concerned about the failed policies in Vietnam; they worried about inflation as the economy was beginning to heat up considerably because of under-financed government spending at home and abroad.

To blunt the impact of such activities, the administration stepped up its public relations offensive in support of its policies in Vietnam. The day that Negotiations Now! was launched, General William Westmoreland, the commander in chief in Vietnam, said that the protests were encouraging the enemy. Richard Nixon, the leading Republican candidate for the 1968 election, had made a similar comment on the day of the New York demonstration. In addition, behind the scenes, the White House helped organize a "Support our Boys in Vietnam" parade that drew 70,000 participants on May 13 in New York. One ad promoting the parade juxtaposed scruffy demonstrators with dead American servicemen.

Even more impressive was the National Committee for Peace and Freedom in Vietnam, which grew out of another behind-the-scenes White House initiative to elicit telegrams supportive of its policy. The committee, headed by former Illinois Democratic senator Paul Douglas and two honorary co-chairs, former presidents Truman and Eisenhower, targeted a "Silent Center" of moderates as its audience. (President Nixon later famously used the similar term "Silent Majority" to rally those who backed his military and political strategies in Vietnam.) John Roche, Johnson's aide who secretly put the Douglas group together, promised the president, "I will leave no tracks."[19] Historians later found the tracks in the archives. When confronted by the evidence, Roche, a former head of the liberal Americans for Democratic Action, saw nothing wrong with his secret role in the allegedly spontaneous development of a citizens' committee.

Despite such relatively successful counter-offensives, some of Johnson's advisers were beginning to worry about how long they could carry on the war before a majority of the population turned against it. In May, Westmoreland revealed his concerns about growing antiwar sentiment when he was confronted with new larger estimates about the size of enemy forces. He chose not to accept those estimates, which suggested that the Communists still had plenty of reserves to contest the United States, primarily because "it will create a political bombshell."[20] Similarly that summer, when he requested another 200,000 troops for the war effort, Johnson rejected the request, fearing a comparable political bombshell. According to one of Westmoreland's aides, in 1967, the general "was under tremendous political pressure to demonstrate progress in the war effort."[21]

Antiwar leaders were not privy to such conversations. In fact, despite the continuing growth of their movement, they were depressed to see how little effect they were having. The war continued with an increasing number of American and Asian casualties, and almost all of North Vietnam was under attack by American bombers, and still there was no end in sight. They would have been cheered had they known that Undersecretary of State Nicholas Katzenbach wondered in November 1967, "Can the tortoise of progress in Vietnam stay ahead of the hare of dissent at home."[22]

ALTHOUGH IT WAS DIFFICULT TO MEASURE, AMERICANS WHO OPPOSED the war in Vietnam were cheered by the support they received from abroad. As the antiwar movement developed in the United States, a large and active antiwar movement was growing in Europe. In the summer of 1967, Bertrand Russell, the great British philosopher and an outspoken opponent of war in general, issued an "Appeal to the American Conscience," to assemble a "Vietnam Tribunal." Held in Sweden, a hotbed of antiwar sentiment and also a neutral in the Cold War, the war crimes trial weighed evidence concerning alleged atrocities Americans were committing in the wars in Southeast Asia. Another of the world's great philosophers, Jean Paul Sartre, served as executive president of the Bertrand Russell Peace Foundation that organized the conference. Russell even invited Johnson to appear to defend his policies and challenge the evidence. Taking the event more seriously than it let on in public, the administration expended considerable energy in successfully discrediting the tribunal and Russell himself.

The American media and most Americans also did not approve of a meeting held in September in Bratislava, a city in Czechoslovakia, which was at that time a Soviet satellite. Forty Americans, including Dellinger, Hayden, and Rennie Davis, met with relatively high-level North Vietnamese and Vietcong officials to discuss ways to end the war. Hayden did not help his cause when he was quoted as saying, "Now we're all Vietcong."[23] The North Vietnamese invited the three Americans to visit their country after the conference. They returned to the United States with three prisoners of war (POWs) as a gesture to the American peace movement and the American people. Other peace activists made similar visits over the next few years to bring

back several more POWs. Many Americans could see through the propaganda message, which suggested that while Washington was incapable
of bringing the captives home, peace activists could do it. Moreover,
while in Vietnam, Americans met with prisoners in staged interviews
and returned to tell the media that, contrary to rumor, they were
humanely treated. That was far from the truth and most Americans suspected as much. In any event, the hobnobbing of peace activists with
Communists abroad and in North Vietnam itself reinforced the administration line that Communists dominated the movement.

Similarly, when frustrated radicals and even revolutionaries in the
movement began talking of escalating their tactics towards more violent confrontations with the government, they did not win many American hearts and minds. At one end of the militant spectrum were pacifists like Dellinger who called for non-violent civil disobedience to
reflect the impatience of the protesters and to increase the costs of
domestic containment. In addition, Dellinger felt that being arrested
for civil disobedience invigorated those who were incarcerated. Jerry
Rubin sounded more radical when he announced in October, "We are
now in the business of wholesale and widespread resistance and dis-
location of American society."[24] Considering more violent tactics, some
members of SDS and SNCC began talking independently about the
prospect of urban guerrilla warfare. They viewed the Newark and
Detroit ghetto disturbances as insurrections that demonstrated the
incendiary nature of American society. Several months later, Bill Ayers,
one of the new cadre of revolutionary SDS leaders, commented that
he thought it possible that the American government could fall "right
now."[25]

Many of the more radical activists, along with liberal representatives, journeyed to Chicago over Labor Day weekend for a National
Conference for a New Politics (NCNP). The 3,000 delegates representing 372 groups made it the largest such gathering since the Progressive
Party convention in 1948. Some who attended discussed building a third-
party movement with Martin Luther King, Jr., who opened the convention and then left, as the presidential candidate. Others looked for
different means to bring about peace and justice at home and abroad.
Despite being in the minority, radicals won the day. The 150-member
Black Caucus threatened to walk out unless the rest of the conference
accepted its demand for 50 percent of the vote. In addition, the caucus led the conference to denounce Zionism, which they claimed was

an imperialist and colonialist philosophy. One disappointed observer saw the floor fight over the Black demands as "a scene worthy of Genet or Pirandello, with whites masquerading as either poor or black, blacks posing as revolutionaries or as arrogant whites, conservatives pretending to be Communists, women feigning to be the oppressed, and liberals pretending not to be there at all."[26]

The key result of the conference was the formation of the NCNP as permanent body, headed by Spock and an African-American leader, James Rollins. Spock used the NCNP as his vehicle to run for president in 1968. The Bratislava and NCNP meetings exacerbated the split between liberals and radicals in the movement and resulted in a dissipation of energies, at least on the national level.

Locally, in the summer and fall of 1967, liberals and pacifists continued their more moderate approaches to ending the war. King and Spock, among others, called for a decentralized "Vietnam Summer" project in which activists would lobby politicians and engage in grassroots education programs to develop a groundswell of support for the antiwar position. Three thousand mostly young people participated in the project that was modeled after the 1964 Mississippi Summer, a civil rights education and voter-registration project. In addition, during the fall, one observer counted at least 110 peace vigils held in communities from Miami, Florida to Everett, Washington. At the same time, thousands of people were engaged in planning for the two major events of the fall, The Resistance's Stop the Draft Week beginning on October 16 and the Mobe's Washington rally on October 21.

THROUGH 1967 THE CALL FOR MORE ORGANIZED AND MILITANT DRAFT resistance grew. SDS members began wearing buttons that read "Resist," a reflection of that group's new line, "From Protest to Resistance." In late September, an unrelated group using the name Resist, published "A Call to Resist Illegitimate Authority" in the *New York Review of Books* and the *New Republic*. Endorsed by M.I.T. linguist Noam Chomsky, author Mary McCarthy, social commentator Paul Goodman, playwright Arthur Miller, Norman Mailer, Benjamin Spock, and over 150 others, the proclamation outlined the illegality and immorality of the war and detailed the ways in which like-minded people could personally resist the draft or support others who did. Five of those who organized the Call were indicted on January 8, 1968, for "conspiring to counsel, aid and abet young men to violate the draft laws." Attorney General Ramsey Clark, something of a civil libertarian, later claimed he indicted the five prominent leaders to enable the movement to present its best case in court. Four of the five were found guilty, with two later acquitted by an appeals court, at which point the Justice Department dropped the charges against the remaining two.

On October 16, the first day of Stop the Draft Week, at least 1,100 men turned in or burned their draft cards in eighteen cities, usually with a sizable crowd of supporters to witness their acts of resistance. In Oakland, 120 resisters were arrested after they employed non-violent civil disobedience in an attempt to close down an induction center. The next day, 3,500 demonstrators attempted the same feat using a bit more force, an action that resulted in counterforce from the police that led to twenty people ending up in the hospital. At a protest about the protest three days later, a wild confrontation occurred between 10,000 demonstrators, some wearing helmets and carrying shields, and 2,000 police officers. The running street battles encouraged revolutionaries who contended that they could successfully defend themselves against the police through new "mobile tactics."

The administration was less troubled by the threat of revolution than by the growing challenges to the draft system and the military itself. In 1967, *New Left Notes* obtained and published a copy of a 1965 Selective Service System document that outlined how to "channel" people into and out of the draft, depending upon their training, in order to maintain the needed number of engineers, scientists, and others in civilian society. Such material aided those who contended the system itself was unfair. The Resistance and others talked about supporting hundreds of thousands of resisters who would weaken the war effort in Vietnam and so clog the courts that few would be ultimately prosecuted.

Johnson's secretary of the army, Stanley Resor, claimed that while he was in office, "The draft delivered enough people without any problem."[27] (Resor's two sons were antiwar activists with student deferments.) On the other hand, in 1967 and 1968, San Francisco's overwhelmed federal prosecutor, dropped 90 percent of the draft cases on his books. In addition, many of the most publicly flagrant resisters escaped the draft because of the fear that they would incite rebellion in the ranks. As late as the first eight months of 1970, even as the war was slowly winding down for Americans, the Selective Service System reported an average of one anti-draft action a day. Such problems helped convince the Nixon Administration to dismantle the draft and adopt an all volunteer army in 1973.

Concerned about the draft pool as early as the summer of 1966, Secretary of Defense McNamara introduced Project 100,000, a program that lowered intelligence standards for recruits in order to fill rising draft quotas without creating more opposition on the campuses. It was sold as an anti-poverty program because the draftees would receive special educational and training classes to improve their skills for return to civilian life. Through 1969, 246,000 young men who would have been otherwise ineligible for the armed services were inducted, 50 percent of whom ended up in Vietnam.

The pool for officers was also drying up. The Reserve Officers Training Corps (ROTC) on college campuses enrolled almost 200,000 students in 1966. Because of the unpopularity of the war, many administrations were forced to end their programs while others that continued were undersubscribed. In 1973, the ROTC program could claim only 72,000 students. Another indicator of the unpopularity of the war was the decline of two collegiate sports powerhouses, the U.S. Military and Naval Academies, which found it increasingly difficult to recruit top high-school athletes, few of whom greeted the prospect of a tour in Vietnam after graduation with much enthusiasm.

The problems in the Selective Service System were exacerbated by an escalation of draft-board break-ins. The military and police could deal with those whose who tried to obstruct induction physically. It was quite another matter to deal with destroyed draft records in an age of relatively primitive information systems. The most famous of the vandals were the Berrigan brothers, Philip and Daniel, Catholic priests deeply committed to ending the war in Vietnam in any way possible. In October 1967, in a symbolic act of civil disobedience, Philip and three colleagues walked into the Customs House in Baltimore, poured blood over draft files while reading from the Bible, and then accepted arrest. The entire operation, which took thirty seconds, did not disrupt the draft system in Baltimore. In 1968, the Baltimore Four received six-year sentences. The following May, in a more sensational break-in, Philip and Daniel and several others, representing the Ultra Resistance, broke into a draft board at Catonsville, Maryland and, in ten minutes, burned 378 files with homemade napalm. One FBI agent complained about Philip, "Him Again! Good God, I'm changing my religion."[28]

Over the next few years, draft-board raiders, often led by priests and other clerics, destroyed records in scores of cities including Los Angeles, Milwaukee, Chicago, Akron, Philadelphia, Indianapolis and four times in New York. In 1971, nine young people stole 32,000 draft files in Buffalo and mailed them to their "owners." At their trial in 1972, the Buffalo Nine were found guilty and sentenced to up to twelve years in jail. Judge John Curtin, however, vacated the sentences saying, "Your love of country is above that of most other citizens. If others had the same sense of morality, the war would have been over a long time ago."[29]

Most troubling was the dissent heard in 1967 from within retired military ranks. Among those to speak out were former Marine Corps commandant David M. Shoup, Rear Admiral Arnold True, General Hugh Hester, and former NATO commander, General Lauris Norstad. J. D. Copping, a navy veteran, burned himself to death in California in August in protest against the war. As for those in active service, Private Andrew Stapp, a draft-card burner who was inducted, began agitating against the war while at Fort Sill, Oklahoma. When he refused to surrender the antiwar literature he distributed to his comrades claiming his First Amendment rights, he was put on trial for disobeying orders. After he and his allies formed the American Servicemen's Union, the Committee for GI Rights, and the first military underground newspaper, *The Bond,* he was discharged from the service.

Over the next few years, draftees and others in Vietnam would breach military discipline, even to the point of refusing to accept orders in a combat zone. In 1969, Company A of the 196th Light Infantry Brigade's Third Battalion participated in the first major mutiny of the war. In 1967 alone, 25,000 military personnel accepted undesirable discharges and for every 100 soldiers, there were seventeen AWOLs and seven desertions. In proportional terms, these totals were the highest in the modern American military. Throughout the armed services, 500,000 of the 7.6 million who served during the Vietnam War era were charged with desertion and over one-half of all personnel were charged with drug offenses, dissidence, or disobedience.

As the campaign season for the 1968 presidential election approached, pressure from those opposed to the continued American presence in the war had become a significant factor in Johnson's military strategies. On the streets of American cities and towns, as well as in the armed services themselves, and on Capitol Hill and in the media, more and more citizens were demanding a speedy resolution of the conflict in Southeast Asia. The North Vietnamese would soon increase that pressure on Lyndon Johnson even more.

NOTES

1. Klein, ed., *Dissent, Power, and Confrontation,* 77.
2. Anderson, *The Movement,* 177.
3. Wells, *The War Within,* 49.
4. Douglas Allen, "Scholars of Asia and the War," in *Coming to Terms: Indochina, the United States, and the War,* eds., Douglas Allen and Ngo Vinh Long (Boulder: Westview, 1991), 234.
5. Barbara L. Tischler, "The Refiner's Fire: Anti-War Activism and Emerging Feminism in the Late 1960's," in *The Vietnam War on Campus: Other Voices, More Distant Drums,* ed., Marc Jason Gilbert (Westport: Praeger, 2001), 57.
6. Rhodri Jeffreys-Jones, *Peace Now! American Society and the Ending of the Vietnam War* (New Haven: Yale University Press, 1999), 104.
7. Lyttle, *Chicago Anti-Vietnam War Movement,* 49.
8. Buzzanco, *Vietnam and the Transformation of American Life,* 2.
9. Wells, *The War Within,* 130.
10. John Morton Blum, *Years of Discord: American Politics and Society, 1961–74* (New York: Norton, 1991), 358.
11. Wells, *The War Within,* 124.
12. DeBenedetti, *An American Ordeal,* 175.
13. Michael Ferber and Staughton Lynd, *The Resistance* (Boston: Beacon, 1971), 90.
14. Anderson, *The Movement,* 268.
15. Murray Polner and Jim O'Grady, *Disarmed and Dangerous: The Radical Lives and Times of Daniel and Philip Berrigan* (New York: Basic, 1997), 266.
16. Jeffreys-Jones, *Peace Now,* 94.
17. Small, *Covering Dissent,* 69.
18. Zaroulis and Sullivan, *Who Spoke Up?* 153.
19. Small, *Johnson, Nixon, and the Doves,* 102.
20. Ibid., 109.
21. Ibid.
22. Anderson, *The Movement,* 163.
23. DeBenedetti, *An American Ordeal,* 192.
24. Ibid., 188.
25. Wells, *The War Within,* 285.
26. DeBenedetti, *An American Ordeal,* 192.

27. Wells, *The War Within*, 268.
28. Polner and O'Grady, *Disarmed and Dangerous*, 198.
29. Heineman, *Campus Wars*, 274.

CHAPTER Five

HEY, HEY, LBJ

R AMSEY CLARK, LYNDON JOHNSON'S ATTORNEY GENERAL, CON-
sidered the October 21–22, 1967 rally in Washington and Pentagon siege "the moment that the fever broke in the whole antiwar movement."[1] The rally and siege set in motion a series of events
that led to the president's speech the following March in which he
rejected further escalation and announced that he would not be a candidate for reelection. It also influenced many other Americans, including a young veteran named Daniel Ellsberg, who watched the siege from
inside the Pentagon.

THE NATIONAL MOBILIZATION COMMITTEE, WHICH HAD DROPPED
Spring from its name in May, planned for the event all through the summer. Considering the massive turnout for the April 15 march in New
York and the pattern that saw each mass demonstration surpassing the
crowd counts of the previous one, organizers of the October rally talked
of attracting as many as one million demonstrators. They did not come
close to that figure—with the most optimistic estimate no more than
75,000. In this case, however, the story was not the size of the crowd
but the intensely dramatic nature of the confrontation.

The Mobe relied heavily on two charismatic veteran activists to put the national demonstration together—David Dellinger, a pacifist who hoped that his movement comrades would begin employing militant non-violent civil disobedience in order to bear witness and to stop the government from being able to wage war, and Jerry Rubin, a master organizer from the West Coast who had shifted from being primarily a political operative to one of the media-designated political spokespersons for the hippie counter-culture. Dellinger's and Rubin's presence in leadership positions, along with the groups that supported them, convinced moderate organizations such as SANE to refuse to co-sponsor the event.

The fear that too large a crowd would produce headlines that could affect public opinion led the administration to launch an all-out offensive against the Mobe. At a cabinet meeting on October 4, Attorney General Ramsey Clark noted that the leadership was made up of a coalition of pacifists and "a heavy representation of extreme left wing groups with long lines of Communist affiliations. . . . The fact of Communist involvement and encouragement," he informed his colleagues, "has been given to some columnists." Not entirely satisfied, the president ordered, "Let's see some more."[2] At a press conference a week later, Secretary of State Dean Rusk assaulted the uninformed and naive academics involved in the demonstrations "who know about enzymes," but little about international affairs.[3] As a precaution, the president ordered a secret deployment of soldiers to the basement of the Commerce Department. So as not to alarm the public or to indicate how seriously the administration took the rally, the soldiers received orders to arrive at the building in civilian clothes driving their own cars. However, they were not needed at the Lincoln Memorial.

"Support Our GI's, Bring Them Home Now!" was the official slogan seen on placards and banners, along with the by-now expected pictures of Ho and Che, and Vietcong flags, that eventful weekend in Washington. The slogan emphasized that antiwar protesters did not oppose the soldiers in Vietnam, only the people in Washington who had sent them there. The day before the October 21 rally at the Lincoln Memorial, young men turned in almost 400 draft cards and enlistment notices at the Justice Department. (It should be pointed out that some of those who turned in or burned their cards maintained duplicates, so that when officials came to arrest them for failing to have a card, they were able to produce one.)

The night before the rally, an evening of speeches at a Washington theater turned into a shambles after a drunken Norman Mailer got up to address the crowd. Mailer soon published a surrealistic memoir of the weekend, *The Armies of the Night: History as a Novel, the Novel as History,* in which as a sort of antihero, he appeared at the center of the events.

The next day a mostly orderly throng gathered at the Memorial to hear speeches from Benjamin Spock, Carl Davidson from SDS, and civil rights activist John Lewis who called for a moment of silence for Che, who had been killed in Bolivia on October 7. The rhetoric was harsher and more radical than at previous demonstrations with Spock, no revolutionary, announcing that the enemy was the president not the Communists in Vietnam. Phil Ochs and Peter, Paul, and Mary were among those who entertained the crowd, although due to an inadequate sound system, those who were not near the platform could barely hear the speeches and the music. One old leftist asked Irving Howe, "In this whole crowd is there anyone but you and I paying attention to what that bastard [Dellinger] is saying?"[4]

Most were able to hear Dellinger when he announced stage two of the protest. Those who wanted more action could join him to march to the Pentagon for a peaceful vigil outside its walls. He had negotiated with government officials about the parade route, where the protesters would stand, and generally what they planned to do. But he warned them he could not control everyone who was coming to Washington. About 35,000 of the participants at the Memorial joined with Dellinger. The vast majority of this contingent was made up of young people led by a few elderly literary celebrities, such as Mailer and the poet Dwight Macdonald. As many as 1,000 radicals, led by a "Revolutionary Contingent," ignored the ground rules and left a rally in a Pentagon parking lot in order to break into the building itself. Over 8,500 members of the 82nd Airborne, who had taken up positions in and around the Pentagon along with local marshals and police, easily rebuffed most of the radicals, although perhaps as many as twenty-five young people breached their defenses and made it to the inside of the building before being arrested.

The rest of the crowd reached their agreed-upon positions outside the Pentagon an hour later, with a minority going somewhat beyond to a plaza in front of the building—an action that apparently violated the agreement between Mobe leaders and the government. For the next few hours, the large band of young people, many of whom sported long hair, torn jeans, and other identifying marks of the hippie culture, confronted a line of short-haired young people in military uniforms. The protesters chanted and shouted obscenities, while a small minority threw eggs, bottles, and even bags of excrement at the soldiers. Several couples engaged in sexual intercourse. In what became a memorable photograph, a young man stuck long-stem flowers into the rifle barrels of the paratroopers in his vicinity. "Make Love Not War" was another popular slogan of the movement.

The colorful Abbie Hoffman, proclaimed by the media a leader of a movement that had no leaders, came to levitate the Pentagon—he claimed that he was successful, that the mystical chants intoned by his followers resulted in the building lifting several feet off the ground. He had earlier promised that it would rise 300 feet during which time all the evil spirits would tumble out. Moreover, he claimed that he had secretly planted a marijuana crop on the Pentagon lawn that would burst into bloom on October 21. Another hippie leader, Jerry Rubin, was arrested for urinating on a Pentagon wall.

During the evening, much of the crowd and almost all of the media began to trickle away from the confrontation line. After midnight and after most journalists had gone home, soldiers cleared the disputed area—using excessive force against the remaining several hundred demonstrators. Several observers reported that some soldiers seemed to have singled out the women for special physical punishment. By Sunday, 667 people had been arrested, the largest number ever arrested at a peace demonstration. Almost all of those arrested went willingly, having planned in advance to do so as part of their civilly disobedient statement against the government. Indeed, Norman Mailer described how difficult it was for him to get arrested; he literally had to ask marshals to do so.

In those days before cable news networks and C-Span, the three major television networks were the only game in town and they chose not to cover even parts of the dramatic demonstration live. Among their arguments were that the appearance of television cameras would affect the nature of the event by causing exhibitionists to act up, and that if they did cover the event, they would have to offer prowar groups equal time. They also contended that even as late as October 1967, antiwar protesters were still a small fringe element in the general population; the vast majority of Americans did not support a minority movement made up, as many concluded, of hippie radicals.

That was clear from the media's reaction to the demonstration. As usual, the dominant element in the coverage was the initial violence at the Pentagon, but not the violent military sweep that took place in the early hours of the morning after the papers had gone to press. James Breslin, the *Washington Post*'s syndicated columnist, captured this disparity in his story headlined, "Bloodied Heads, Bloodied Cause: Quiet Rally Turns Vicious," while the respected *New York Times* columnist James Reston commented under a story headed, "Everyone is a Loser/ Washington is a Sad and Brooding City in the Wake of the Antiwar Demonstration." According to them, everything was going well until radicals provoked violence at the Pentagon. The UPI's influential Merriman Smith was "depressed" by what he saw at the Pentagon, "hippies, Vietcong flags, foul language and manners," while *Time* referred to Dellinger as a "mob leader."[5] Although buried in most stories was the fact that the demonstrators at the Lincoln Memorial were generally decorous and law-abiding, most Americans saw and read pictures and accounts about marijuana- or acid-using hippies who had no respect for authority or for middle-class values. Journalists were helped with graphic stories leaked from the White House, on the president's orders, about demonstrators who urinated and engaged in sexual intercourse in public.

NINETEEN SIXTY-SEVEN WAS THE YEAR THAT ALMOST EVERYONE IN THE United States learned about the hippie phenomenon. San Francisco's Haight-Ashbury district was the magnet, drawing thousands of bearded, long-haired, sandal-clad youthful dropouts to a "Summer of Love." No one apparently needed money to enjoy it. Everyone loved everyone so much that clothing, food, shelter, and drugs were all free.

People looking and behaving like what came to be called hippies first appeared on the scene around 1965. For lack of a better word, journalists initially referred to them as "beatniks," cultural rebels of the late '50s who read poetry, drank wine, lived in Greenwich Village and North Beach, and rejected materialism. Herb Caen, a San Francisco columnist, invented the word "hippie" in 1965 because he considered the new bohemians to be hip or hipsters.

Young people who looked like hippies first began appearing in significant numbers at political demonstrations in 1966, calling for "flower power" and supporting the Marxism of Groucho. They also had their own cultural happenings, or Be-In's, the most famous of which was in San Francisco's Golden Gate Park in January, 1967, where their favorite band, the Grateful Dead, performed. Hippies also adopted the flip attitudes and, especially, the funky clothing sported by another of their favorite musical groups, the Beatles, whose 1966 song and film, "Yellow Submarine," they much admired. By 1968, there were probably 200,000 full-time hippies who lived counter-cultural lives in rural and urban communes, perhaps another 300,000 who shared their beliefs, and as many as 3 million who might be considered sympathizers or weekend hippies. Many opposed Amerika's "Death Culture," supported drug guru Dr. Timothy Leary who contended "Your only hope is dope," and who urged them to "Tune in, turn on, and drop out." "Do your own thing" and "Question Authority," were the sorts of slogans that appeared on their tie-dyed T-shirts and on bumper stickers on beat-up Volkswagen buses.

Hippies generally came to the demonstrations for the music and had little interest in the left-wing politics of the antiwar coalitions. In January 1968, however, a handful of pranksters, including Abbie Hoffman and Jerry Rubin, formed a Yippie Party that blended pot and politics. But they were not really serious—Rubin wrote that "The secret to the Yippie myth is that it is nonsense," and its slogan, "Rise up and abandon the creeping meatball" meant nothing at all.[6] Tom Hayden, who often found himself in conflict with hippies and yippies in the antiwar van, considered their "movement" to be "absurdity masquerading as revolutionary politics."[7] It is true, however, that the great hippie musical "Hair," which opened in April 1968 proclaiming the Age of Aquarius, did have a solid political message.

Most Americans did not like hippies and their culture. Many parents feared that their own children might become dope-smoking, free-loving hippies. By the time of the siege of the Pentagon, many antiwar demonstrators, even if they did not adhere completely to the mores of hippiedom, looked like hippies. Many young people, and even some of their elders, who marched against the war wore long hair, sneakers or sandals, and often torn T-shirts or jeans, shouted lewd chants, were not averse to promiscuity, and saw nothing wrong with taking a puff from a marijuana cigarette when offered one. Sometimes they sewed an upside-down American flag on their jeans, a practice that led the House to pass legislation that made it a federal crime to mutilate or desecrate the flag, punishable with up to a one-year term in jail and a fine of $1,000.

For many Americans by 1967, antiwar demonstrators were not only unruly and potentially violent but hippies, whose life-style was even more threatening and a greater offense to middle-class sensibilities than was their advocacy of left-wing political causes. Thus, because of what they wore and the people with whom they hung out, serious politically oriented activists became easily conflated with hippies to the detriment of their cause.

THERE WAS NO DOUBT THAT THE ADMINISTRATION WAS CONCERNED about the rally and march to the Pentagon on October 21–22. On the first day, the president received almost hourly reports about what the protesters were doing. He heard that some at the Pentagon carried signs that read "LBJ sucks," "LBJ pull out like your father should have done," and "I'd rather fuck than fight."[8] Overall, he was pleased with the way the media had handled the event. In the weeks following the demonstration, as had been the case previously, the ratio of dovish to hawkish letters to the White House on the war narrowed and the president's approval ratings improved.

Although fewer than 75,000 people showed up for the main rally and only half that number for the march to the Pentagon, and although the press stressed demonstrator violence and hippie behavior, anti-warriors enjoyed a symbolic success when pictures of their siege were published in electronic and print media around the world. The specter of American citizens surrounding the center of their war-making machine presented a powerful image of a nation in turmoil. The siege of the Pentagon was an example of why early SDS leader and later chronicler of the sixties, Todd Gitlin, described the antiwar movement as "a marvel of inventiveness."[9]

The administration was feeling the heat, if not from the unpopular Pentagon demonstration, then certainly from the growing number of politicians, intellectuals, and journalists who were not only concerned about the war but also about the disruption in society and the alienation of young people—often young people from their families or families down the street in their upper-and upper-middle class neighborhoods. The nation appeared to be falling apart, as demonstrated by the unprecedented clash at the Pentagon.

Although it was unknown to the public at the time, Secretary of Defense McNamara was one of those inside the government who had become disillusioned with the war. He had offered a rather pessimistic military review to a Senate Committee in August that was so at odds with what his generals and admirals believed that he came close to provoking the first resignation of the Joint Chiefs of Staff in American history. During that same period, Robert Kennedy had urged him on several occasions to resign and break publicly with the administration. On November 1, he submitted to the president another pessimistic Vietnam report that looked a good deal like a resignation. Johnson, who had been worried earlier about the emotional health of his secretary of defense, was worried even more about his lack of enthusiasm for pursuing the war. Although McNamara stayed on at Defense as an informal lame duck until February 1, Johnson soon arranged for him to assume the presidency of the World Bank.

On the same day that he received the report from McNamara, the president met with his "Wise Men," an informal bipartisan advisory group that included distinguished former government officials and military officers. Unlike McNamara, all of them, except for George Ball, expressed confidence in the path the administration was taking. They did express concern, however, about the erosion of public support for the war. McGeorge Bundy spoke for many there, including the president himself, when he wrote to his former boss a week after the meeting. "Public discontent with the war is now wide and deep. One of the few things that helps us right now is public distaste for the violent doves—but I think people are really getting fed up with the endlessness of the fighting."[10]

Instead of devising a new military strategy that might bring the war to a speedy end, and, in fact, believing that General Westmoreland's tactics were grinding the enemy down, Johnson decided to deal with opinion problem through a new public relations campaign. He summoned Westmoreland home, along with U.S. ambassador to South Vietnam, Ellsworth Bunker, to offer a series of speeches and press conferences in November assuring the nation that things were going well in Vietnam and that there was light at the end of the proverbial tunnel. The president himself went on the hustings to echo that theme and also to caution doves gently that they were making it more difficult to end the war because of the encouragement they gave to Hanoi. Johnson was too much of a civil libertarian to launch the all-out war against dissenters that President Nixon began two years later.

The public relations blitz turned out to be a monumental blunder. The administration had been under attack by dissenters from the Right and Left for having a credibility problem. When the Communists launched their Tet Offensive on January 31, 1968, their early victories, including seizing part of the Saigon embassy compound, gave lie to the optimistic progress reports Americans had heard only three months earlier.

But that was well after Johnson received support from his Wise Men in November and in December a poll revealed support for escalation over withdrawal at a 63–37 margin. He was not especially concerned when he received intelligence reports that at an informal retreat hosted by FOR in November, representatives of the Fifth Avenue Peace Parade Committee, SDS, SNCC, CORE, radical pacifists, and others endorsed civil disobedience, although they urged those who practiced it to avoid the sort of violence that their colleagues had met with at the Pentagon. The turn toward more radical strategies had an ambiguous and complicated impact on the effectiveness of the antiwar movement. Some observers later argued that this tactical shift on the part of some doves made it more difficult to attract moderates to their position. Others claimed that by creating more instability in society, they caused many more Americans to demand an end to the war in order to end the instability.

ONLY SLIGHTLY MORE TROUBLING TO JOHNSON THAN THE DISSENTERS' tactical shift was the announcement on November 30 that Senator Eugene McCarthy was entering the Democratic primaries to run against him. In his announcement of candidacy, McCarthy linked the underfinanced failing War on Poverty, the decline of non-military foreign aid, inflation, and the alienation of youth to the war, which, if elected, he would end promptly. But not enough states had primaries in 1968 to guarantee that the victor in that campaign would gain the nomination at a convention controlled by politicians beholden to the president. More important, McCarthy was one of the more obscure senators and not an especially charismatic campaigner. Some of his supporters were seen sleeping during his less-than-arousing keynote speech at a late December conference. The *Village Voice* sadly reported that his speeches were "dull and vague, without either poetry or balls."[11] How he became the dove's candidate demonstrates the relative strength of the president's position, even in the fall of 1967.

After the 1966 elections, in which the Democratic Party suffered significant defeats, liberal party activists Allard Lowenstein and Curtis Gans took the lead in forming a "Dump Johnson" movement. They wanted to offer an option to antiwar Democrats between the president and the left sectarians who dominated the leadership of the antiwar movement. Working with antiwar Committees of Concerned Democrats that sprouted up in many states in 1967, Lowenstein and Gans searched for a viable candidate to challenge Johnson. They pressed Senator Robert F. Kennedy in particular because, inheriting the Kennedy machine and legacy, he would have been the most powerful candidate. Kennedy, who had broken with the president over Vietnam in February and who had never enjoyed good relations with him, rejected their many entreaties, arguing that he did not want to turn the Vietnam issue into a personal contest between himself and Johnson. With leadership cadres behind them and the promise of funding, Lowenstein and Gans sought out numerous prominent dovish senators and other office holders looking for someone to take up their mantle. The Dump Johnson movement was virtually down to its last choices when McCarthy, who felt very strongly about the war, agreed to be their candidate.

McCarthy was a highly intelligent, thoughtful politician who wrote poetry. But he looked like a long shot when after a month of campaigning, Johnson led him in the polls 63 to 17 percent. He had less than two months to close the gap in the first primary of the year in New Hampshire. Endorsements from SANE in January and the Americans for Democratic Action in February helped, but those organizations had few adherents in New Hampshire.

The ever-resourceful antiwar leaders behind the insurgency did not have the money or the political connections of the administration which had begun a write-in campaign to challenge McCarthy since the president had not even entered the primary. The McCarthy campaign counted on "People Power," especially college students who trooped to New Hampshire as they once trooped to the South for voter-registration drives. Understanding American politics, many of those who rang doorbells and handed out leaflets at the supermarkets became "Clean for Gene"—they shaved off their beards, cut their hair, and put on coats and ties and dresses and heels.

THE COLLEGES WERE THE MAJOR SOURCE FOR FOOT SOLDIERS FOR THE antiwar movement. As recently as 1964, University of California president Clark Kerr, a liberal, had responded to Berkeley's Free Speech Movement (FSM) by proclaiming, that the "university is an educational institution that has been given to the regents as a trust to administer for educational reasons, and not to be used for direct political action." The FSM's Mario Savio, who saw the university as "the place where people begin seriously to question the conditions of their existence," rejected Kerr's position. In respect to experienced educational leaders like Kerr, Savio's colleague, Jack Weinberg, may have been the one to coin the slogan, "Don't trust anyone over thirty."[12] As one observer of the Berkeley events of the winter of 1964 commented, the FSM revealed "the intriguing possibilities of a radical left constituency composed exclusively of students."[13] By the end of 1967, according to one poll, 19 percent of college students believed there was a need in the United States for a mass revolutionary party.

College students were agitated over many things, including paternalistic administrations and rigid curriculums. In the early sixties, many college administrations enforced dress codes and curfews for coeds, and some even sent students' grades to their parents. The key issues then on campus involved those related to *in loco parentis;* off campus it was civil rights. But by the late sixties, in part because many of the *in loco parentis* practices had been dropped, students were most concerned about the war and the draft and related issues of classified research and recruiting for the military and military industries on campus.

Between 1960 and 1970, the percentage of young people between the ages of 18 and 21 attending college had risen from 23 to 35 percent. For the first time in American history, the number of college students surpassed the number of farmers. The number of faculty grew from almost 2.5 million in 1955 to almost 6.5 million in 1970, while the number of graduate students grew from 242,000 to 816,000 during the same period. In addition, from 1960 to 1970, the median age of Americans had dropped from 29.5 to 28.

Much of the increase in enrollment took place on large state university campuses such as Michigan State, Penn State, and Kansas, public institutions where administrators, state legislatures, and governors were less patient with protesters than private schools such as Columbia and Harvard. Governor Ronald Reagan of California, for example, shut down all of his campuses for four days after rioting broke out in May 1970, while governors called out the National Guard in Kentucky, South Carolina, Illinois, Wisconsin, and Ohio, among other states, to contain rioters at state universities. Further, state legislators in 40 states in 1969 and 1970 introduced tough legislation to curb campus extremism. Ivy League campuses did not have to deal with state legislatures.

A good deal of the growth of the state universities was related to contracts for government-sponsored research that soon became a sore point with some students. Under Project Themis, the government distributed research grants for military research to many state universities. In 1948, fifty-seven faculty nationwide were in some way recipients of grants for military research; that number reached 500,000 by 1968. That same year, universities spent $3 billion on research projects, 70 percent of which came from the federal government, and half of that amount was defense-related; that is, one in three research dollars was defense-related. At the University of Michigan, the figure was 43 percent.

With new resources from the government, Michigan State, for example, not only expanded its enrollment but also became one of the leaders in funding Merit Scholars, many of whom were budding intellectuals who participated in political organizations on that once bucolic agricultural school. Not all of them turned to the left. The University Christian Movement was founded on the East Lansing campus in 1966, the same year that campus radicals made good use of the *Ramparts* article that revealed their university's role in the training of brutal South Vietnamese police personnel. While SDS boasted 100,000 members in 1968—the year before it was to destroy itself in a paroxysm of sectarian violence—the conservative Young Americans for Freedom (YAF), founded in 1960 with 20,000 members in twenty-five chapters, reached 50,000 members and 500 chapters in only five years. But many of these organizations, particularly those on the left, were rather loosely run from campus to campus. Speaking of his group in Berkeley, Jerry Rubin observed that "any lunatic could walk in off the street, write a leaflet, mimeograph it, sign it 'Vietnam Day Committee' and pass it out."[14]

Overall, of the more than 2,500 universities and colleges, only 10 percent experienced violent disturbances during the war, and on those campuses, fewer than 10 percent of students were activists. But the numbers of demonstrations and activists on campus were less important than the attention they received from the media and the general sympathy they enjoyed from many students and faculty members.

Although YAF members sometimes engaged in unruly protests, most of the lawbreaking, civil disobedience, and violence came from the Left. Tom Hayden claims that from 1965 to 1971, 26,358 students were arrested on campus, fourteen were killed, thousands were injured, and thousands more expelled. In 1969, 77 percent of the faculty in one poll supported the idea of expelling student disrupters. They were reacting to an escalation in campus violence as the war escalated in South Vietnam.

There were 71 demonstrations involving at least thirty-five people each on sixty-two campuses during the fall 1967 semester. Those numbers rose to 221 on 101 campuses during the winter 1968 semester. At Berkeley alone during the 1968–69 school year, there were six major confrontations between students and the police, which resulted in twenty-two days of street fighting, 2,000 arrests, 150 suspensions or expulsions, and twenty-two days of occupation by the National Guard. Just across the Bay Bridge, beginning in December 1968, San Francisco State University experienced a 134-day strike, initially over curriculum issues, during which time only one-third of the classes were able to meet. The tough tactics of the president of the university, prominent semanticist S. I. Hayakawa, catapulted him to the Senate in 1976.

Columbia University, in the media center of the United States, was the setting for one of the most important and violent clashes of the era. Aside from the war, protesters were concerned about classified research and the ways the university interacted with the local African-American community. The administration had been unresponsive to several years of peaceful agitation from students, some of whom finally became impatient for reform. For seven days in April 1968, hundreds of radical students occupied five campus buildings, including the president's office (which they declared with a sign from his window to be "Liberated Area"), formed revolutionary committees and communes, held a dean hostage for twenty-four hours, and wrote on walls, "Create two, three, many Columbia's" a play on the Cuban revolutionaries' call to create many Cubas in the hemisphere. Tom Hayden boasted, "Students at last, had taken power in their own hands."[15] One Black militant, who saw Columbia as the nearest and easiest target in the establishment, explained, "There's one oppressor—in the White House, in [Columbia's] Low Library, in Albany, New York. You strike a blow at Low Library, you strike a blow for Freedom Fighters in Angola, Mozambique, Portuguese Guinea, Zimbabwe, South Africa."[16]

After exhibiting considerable patience while the radicals smoked the presidents' cigars and carted off his papers, university officials called in the New York police who violently routed the protesters from the buildings. This action led to 700 arrests and 120 charges of police brutality, including several involving attacks on faculty who were serving as peace-keeping marshals. Without condoning violence or the sort of lawbreaking that students committed at Columbia, Kenneth Keniston, a prominent sociologist, considered "the radicalism of a minority of today's college students a largely appropriate, reasonable and measured response to blatant injustice."[17] More than three decades later, another scholar, Joel P. Rhodes concluded that "violent performances against the symbols of the American system proved the most economical and visually arresting way of immediately achieving a symbolic victory over ... more powerful adversaries." He found the use of violence during the era to be a "rational and viable ... method of political discourse."[18] Perhaps, but it certainly was not the best way to "make friends and influence people" among the great American middle class.

Young faculty and especially graduate students often led the undergraduates. There were wide variations in political positions among the faculty from campus to campus, and especially, from discipline to discipline. In a study of 60,000 faculty done during the period, 5.1 percent claimed they were radical, 41.5 percent accepted a liberal label, while 27.7 percent called themselves conservative. But only 12 percent of social scientists said they were conservative compared to 41 percent of the engineering faculty.

The actual number of students and faculty involved in antiwar and other left-wing movements on campus is not as important as the nature of the leftist political culture on specific campuses. It is here that the antiwar movement and New Left ultimately affected policy, because as the sons and daughters of the upper-middle and upper classes, the children of the establishment, became radicals or hippies or both, their parents paid attention. In the highest policymaking circles in the Johnson (and later Nixon) administrations, some of the children and young relatives of McNamara, Katzenbach, Resor, the Bundy brothers, Rusk, and Paul Nitze and Paul Warnke of the Defense Department had become opponents of the war. In what one observer labeled "child stealing," they and others like them had been targeted by activists as children of influential parents who, if convinced to join the movement, would affect their parents' views of the war.[19] State Department official Marshall Green remembered, "*All* of us . . . had sons or daughters who were involved in this, I mean, everybody did."[20]

Leaders of the American establishment, including Johnson's Wise Men, did not have to have a radical child to realize by 1968 that if the war went on much longer, there might not be another establishment generation, for many of the young people at Harvard, Columbia, and Stanford were not going to go on for an MBA or to law school, Wall Street, or government service. Of the student radicals, Nitze complained, "They were against the whole goddam show. They wanted to tear it down. That's the kind of thing I worried about."[21]

It became difficult if not impossible for government leaders and candidates to appear on campuses. During the 1968 campaign, Richard Nixon's speech at the University of Akron in early October was successfully disrupted by at least 200 members of the audience chanting "Ho, Ho, Ho Chi Minh, Ho Chi Minh is gonna win," while an SDS member yelled "Sieg Heil" and one student shouted, "You fucking asshole."[22] In the long run, though, Nixon could not deliver his speech as intended, the uncivil behavior worked to his benefit as the candidate who would restore "law and order."

But that situation was far off. In early 1968, with the insurgency of Eugene McCarthy an implausible one, Lyndon Johnson appeared to be a formidable Democratic candidate if he could keep his party together on the issue of Vietnam. Then came Tet. The Communists had been taking a beating from Westmoreland's search-and-destroy strategy of attrition in South Vietnam and from air attacks on North Vietnam during 1966 and 1967. But they were far from being beaten. Nonetheless, considering the toll the war was taking on them, they decided to launch a nationwide conventional offensive during the lunar New Year holiday, Tet, starting on January 31, expecting hundreds of thousands of South Vietnamese to rally to their flag.

American intelligence had expected an offensive but not of the size and intensity as that launched by Hanoi. Initially, the Vietcong and the North Vietnamese forces made significant gains, including the takeover of Hue, South Vietnam's imperial capital, and especially, a brief penetration of the American embassy in Saigon, an event captured by U.S. television cameras. But the Communists had miscalculated—there was no nationwide uprising to support them and, in a matter of days, the tide of battle had turned. By the end of February 1968, it was clear they had suffered a bloody and costly defeat. They were able to wreak a good deal of havoc in the countryside, destroying pacification programs and South Vietnamese governmental infrastructures, but they were on the run. Yet when Johnson proclaimed victory, few Americans believed him. And rightly so since Tet, the turning point of the war, was a signal psychological victory for the Communists.

Americans saw Vietnamese sappers inside a building in the embassy compound. They also heard an American officer calling in artillery to pummel a village taken by the Vietcong, informing his listeners stateside, "We had to destroy it, in order to save it."[23] And most important, they saw the chief of police of Saigon execute a helpless prisoner on a street in the capital. Like the rest of the nation, when NBC's John Chancellor and a producer first saw the film of the execution, they just "sat in shock."[24] The Saigon chief suspected that the enemy soldier was one of those who had shot up a building housing unarmed women, children, and dependents of South Vietnamese officials. But Americans did not know that and it probably would not have mattered very much to many of them.

As expected during a perceived crisis, in the wake of Tet, Americans told pollsters they supported their president. But that response was only a temporary one. All through the war, Americans had been asked whether they thought getting involved in Vietnam had been a mistake. In the weeks after Tet, for the first time more than 50 percent of those polled responded affirmatively to that question. That percentage would continue to rise through the Nixon administration as well.

During the first week of the Tet Offensive, CALCAV arrived in Washington for lobbying and silent vigils. At one of those ecumenical vigils, Rabbi Abraham Heschel broke the silence to cry out, "My God, my God, why hast thou forsaken me," Christ's lament. During the same period, prominent antiwar professor Seymour Melman made headlines with his 400-page moral critique of U.S. conduct in the war, *In the Name of America*. Pressure, no longer created by the activists alone, was building.

Tet sent shockwaves through the entire American political and economic system. Clark Clifford, who took over the Pentagon from McNamara on February 1, called for a review of Vietnam policy as he and his colleagues considered their recommendations to the president about the course to pursue after the Communist offensive. Clifford, a respected

Democratic leader since his service in the Truman administration, had been a loyal supporter of the president's Vietnam policies since 1965, despite some initial doubts. Now he began to harbor new ones.

Most of his military chieftains, convinced they had the enemy on the run, supported a call for an additional 206,000 troops, to join the 550,000 already there, to back up an aggressive offensive that promised military victory. Clifford and his aides had to weigh that request against the growing opposition to the war. When he became convinced that even with another 206,000 troops the military had no satisfactory plan to end the war with dispatch, Clifford became a secret dove, working with like-minded colleagues in a cabal to convince the president to reject the escalation option. The war was tearing the country apart—with its impact felt from Wall Street to Main Street.

When the president called his Wise Men to the White House on March 25 and 26, he was shocked that almost all of them had turned 180 degrees from the positions they had held the previous November. Furious, he asked George Ball, "Who the hell brainwashed those friends of yours."[25] Five days later, appearing on national television, Johnson announced that he was cutting back on the bombing of North Vietnam as an inducement to Hanoi to enter into negotiations. He was not happy about it, complaining privately, "I'll tell you what happens when there is a bombing halt. I halt and then Ho Chi Minh shoves his trucks right up my ass."[26]

Even more important, the president shocked the nation by announcing that he had decided not to run for reelection so that he could devote all of his time to ending the war. Further, he made no commitment to send hundreds of thousands of more troops to Vietnam, as his military had requested. After this speech, hundreds of thousands of college students poured out of their dormitories, celebrating their great victory with chants, "The hawk is dead." Looking back at the epochal speech two years later, Norman Mailer asked, "Which one of us thought Johnson would cave in. . . . the man was suffering from the barrage we were giving him."[27] The antiwarriors exaggerated their role in compelling Johnson to make the decisions that so pleased them, but they did play a central role.

Johnson came to those decisions because of a variety of factors. Although he was certain he could have gained the nomination of his party for the presidency, he was concerned about his close victory in the popular vote over McCarthy in New Hampshire and the entry of

Robert Kennedy into the race after McCarthy's strong showing. Moreover, the president worried about the effects of the war on the economy with inflation on the rise and a concomitant threatened run on
the Treasury's gold reserves by nervous Europeans. Like Clifford, he
also had lost confidence in his military chieftains' ability to bring an
end to the war in a reasonable period of time. Even had he accepted
their proposals, he had to be concerned about where he was going to
get the additional troops they claimed to need to get the job done—
from the draft, which was encountering more and more resistance or
from calling up the National Guard and the Reserves, which many
middle-class young people were using as a refuge from the battle zone?

The rhetorical and even physical attacks on the Selective Service
System were only one reflection of the alienation of many young people from their government's policies in Vietnam. As one contemporary observer noted, the war in Vietnam had become "the central fact
in the life of an entire generation."[28] The country appeared to be
falling apart and the war was the main cause. Beginning as a tiny
cloud on the horizon in 1965, the antiwar movement had grown
impressively to a point at which its arguments had been adopted by
many people who would never have participated in a demonstration
or signed a petition. In a complicated symbiotic relationship, antiwar
activists affected and were affected by prominent figures in Congress,
the media, and the intellectual world who confronted the president
with an articulate, sizable, and increasingly influential group of citizens whose proposals for withdrawal from Vietnam began to appear
more credible than those of the president who could only promise
more of the same.

The antiwar movement had taken a toll on Johnson personally. A
gregarious politician who enjoyed traveling around the country as president and pressing the flesh, he could no longer appear in public without hearing foul-mouthed chanters or seeing displeasing placards about
"Johnson's War." He was the first president to confront such visible
and unruly opposition. Indeed, barely a day went by after 1965 when
there were not at least a few protesters chanting outside the window
of the official residence, "Hey, Hey LBJ, How Many Kids Did You Kill
Today?" In fact, for eight years, Women for Peace showed up every
Saturday at the White House from 11 to 1 for a peace vigil that
involved as few as four demonstrators and as many as 30. One can
imagine that as the red lights faded on the television cameras on March

31, 1968, he breathed a sigh of relief; he and his family would no longer be personal targets of the unruly and uncivil demonstrators.

BEGINNING WITH THE PENTAGON SIEGE THE PREVIOUS OCTOBER AND the related public relations campaign to sell the war in November, the antiwar movement and antiwar critics were among the several important elements that drove Johnson to make his momentous announcements at the end of March 1968. There was some legitimacy in the students' boasts that they had killed the hawk. But while the president had decided not to escalate and to make it easier for the Communists to accept his invitation to negotiate, the war was not going to come to any sudden end. Moreover, the president's decision not to run did not guarantee that the Democrats would nominate an antiwar candidate. A few weeks after Johnson's speech, his liberal vice president, Hubert H. Humphrey, threw his hat in the ring vowing to continue administration policies. Although a skeptic on the war in 1965, Humphrey soon learned not to disagree with Johnson—who froze him out for several weeks on one occasion when it appeared that he was dissenting from official policy. In 1968 he understood clearly that if he wanted the full support of the party machinery during the campaign, he had to remain on the relatively short leash held firmly by the president. The movement's battles were not yet over.

NOTES

1. Small, *Johnson, Nixon, and the Doves*, 110.
2. Ibid., 112.
3. Ibid., 113.
4. Howe, *A Margin of Hope*, 305–6.
5. Small, *Covering Dissent*, 78, 79.
6. Rubin, *Do It!* 83.
7. Hayden, *Reunion*, 204.
8. Small, *Covering Dissent*, 82–83.
9. Wells, *The War Within*, xvii.
10. Small, *Johnson, Nixon, and the Doves*, 121.
11. Anderson, *The Movement*, 189.
12. Ibid., 105, 106.
13. Willis Rudy, *The Campus and a Nation in Crisis: From the American Revolution to Vietnam* (Madison, NJ: Associated University Presses, 1996), 153.

14. Rubin, *Do It!* 37.

15. Hayden, *Reunion,* 274.

16. Anderson, *The Movement,* 195.

17. Blum, *Years of Discord,* 361.

18. Joel P. Rhodes, *The Voice of Violence: Performative Violence as Protest in the Vietnam Era* (New York: Praeger, 2001), 3, 187.

19. Jeffreys-Jones, *Peace Now!* 53.

20. Wells, *The War at Home,* 373.

21. Ibid., *The War Within,* 247.

22. Heineman, *Campus Wars,* 223.

23. Anderson, *The Movement,* 184.

24. Clarence R. Wyatt, *Paper Soldiers: The American Press and the Vietnam War* (New York: Norton, 1993), 166.

25. Wells, *The War Within,* 251.

26. Ibid., 252.

27. Klein, ed., *Dissent, Power, and Confrontation,* 49.

28. Powers, *The War at Home,* xix.

CHAPTER Six

CONFRONTING NIXON

$\mathbf{A}$LTHOUGH THE NORTH VIETNAMESE AND NLF WERE BATTERED
in the weeks after Tet and talks were under way from May
through December in Paris about setting up formal negotiations, 1968 was the bloodiest year of the entire Vietnam War for American troops, with battle deaths rising from 9,500 in 1967 to over
14,500. It was also a bloody year on the home front as frustrated radicals took to the streets in ever more militant actions as they saw their
apparent victory of March 31 begin to slip away. Even the mild-man-
nered clerics of CALCAV displayed their growing militancy when several of their number broke into a Dow Chemical meeting in Midland,
Michigan on May 8.

FIVE DAYS AFTER JOHNSON DELIVERED HIS EPOCHAL SPEECH, DR. Martin Luther King, Jr., was assassinated. His murder precipitated riots
in many cities, including Washington. In Chicago, Mayor Richard
Daley took an especially tough line towards rioters, an action that
also served as a warning to protesters who were intending to visit in
August, when his city was to host the Democratic National Convention. He instructed his police to "shoot to kill arsonists and shoot to

maim looters." Attorney General Ramsey Clark responded, "That's murder, and if you're not indicted in Cook County, we'll indict you for civil rights violations."[1]

The rioting in the aftermath of King's assassination, as well as Johnson's March 31 announcements, helped keep the crowds down at the by-now routine spring antiwar demonstrations. On Friday, April 26, the Student Mobe declared a nationwide strike for high school and college students that resulted in as many as 200,000 young people, most of whom were from the New York area, skipping school that day. On Saturday, April 27, Mobe demonstrations in New York and San Francisco drew 100,000 and 20,000 participants respectively. Although the New York crowd was not as large as the one that marched to the United Nations the previous spring, it far outnumbered the relative handful of people who showed up for the Loyalty Day parade on the same day. Nonetheless, the media took a decided disinterest in the antiwar activities that weekend, in part because, aside from the strike, they offered nothing new and, more important, why pay attention to antiwar demonstrators when it appeared that the nation was on its way to ending the war through negotiations. Moreover, two antiwar Democratic candidates were riding high in the primaries.

Many activists who might have thrown themselves into demonstrations were working on the McCarthy and Kennedy campaigns in the spring of 1968. The problem was that winning the primaries was no guarantee; not enough states held primaries to insure a victory at the convention. There Johnson's candidate, Vice President Humphrey, who did not win any primaries, would have enough delegates elected from party conventions and caucuses to secure the nomination. The antiwar Democrats' only hope was to convince uncommitted delegates through their campaigns and from polling that only they could win the election in November. McCarthy was a rather colorless one-issue candidate who was an indifferent and even indolent campaigner. Kennedy attracted a broader base of support, particularly among those committed to maintaining and extending Great Society reforms. But on June 5, almost two months to the date of King's assassination, Kennedy was assassinated on the night of his victory over McCarthy in the California primary.

Antiwar activists began planning in the spring for demonstrations at the Democratic convention. Some even talked of bringing 200,000 protesters to Chicago to make known to the delegates their dissatisfaction with a Humphrey candidacy and a Vietnam plank in the party's platform—dictated by the president. The Mobe decided against sponsoring the protests because its leaders feared they would attract militant activists whose actions would provoke a violent response from Mayor Daley. Veteran antiwar leaders Dellinger, Davis, and Hayden played the major role in organizing the events, opening a Chicago office as early as February. Dellinger and Davis were committed to non-violence, but Hayden had begun talking like a Black Panther, vowing to combat the authorities if they became violent. He proclaimed, "To call a man a 'pig' is not a provocation of the same scale as the use and display of automatic weapons."[2] Hayden later reported that he "expected violence . . . but we would not initiate it ourselves."[3]

A wild card were the Yippies, a mostly phantom organization led by the media-savvy Abbie Hoffman and Jerry Rubin, who enjoyed threatening Mayor Daley and the delegates with bizarre and surreal actions. They planned to nominate a pig named "Pigasus" for president at their Festival of Life. They also promised wholesale fornication in the public parks, releasing greased pigs through the streets of Chicago, employing Yippie hookers to entrap delegates, burning 100,000 draft cards, hosting a float-in of 10,000 nude swimmers, and lacing the Chicago water supply with LSD, a hallucinogenic drug. Rubin was quoted as saying "Radicalization involves smoking dope in the park and fighting the pigs [police] in the street."[4] Most serious politicos did not support the fanciful plans and non-existent political platform of the Yippie pranksters, but the Chicago authorities were nervous, especially about the possibility of LSD in their water supply. Most Americans who read about the "antiwar protesters" called Yippies were not amused by the threats that they and Mayor Daley took seriously.

The combination of fear of Daley's police and the likelihood of violent confrontations, plus the tactics employed by the mayor to make it difficult for demonstrators to hold legal protests (city hall refused to issue permits for parades or for musicians who would draw crowds), prompted only 10,000 demonstrators to show up during the convention from August 25 through August 30, and that figure included 5,000 young people from the Chicago area. But those 10,000, along with Mayor Daley, the FBI, and Democratic Party officials, made the Chicago convention the most notorious political convention in American history.

Inside the hall, the Humphrey forces, who controlled more than enough delegates to secure the nomination despite his failure to win one primary, rejected a moderately dovish Vietnam plank. Instead, they went "all the way with LBJ," who demanded no direct or oblique criticism of his Vietnam policy. Many Democratic doves would have supported Humphrey had he run on a Vietnam plank that offered the possibility of a change in policy. Humphrey wanted to appeal to the doves with such a plank, but the proud Johnson refused to permit him to meet them half way.

Mayor Daley ran the convention with an iron fist, protecting delegates from invasion from the streets with repressive security measures, while taking advantage of a convenient electricians' strike to make it difficult for television reporters to cover the proceedings inside and outside the halls. In describing the mayor's media relations, *Newsweek* headed its story, "Beat the Press." In fact, police and security guards on the convention floor roughed up several prominent journalists—in full view of television cameras. Sixty-three newspeople claimed to have been injured in the hall or on the streets covering demonstrations. The Chicago police had orders to go after journalists and photographers who were documenting their illegal actions. On one occasion, when Connecticut senator Abraham Ribicoff criticized the tactics of Chicago security forces from the convention platform, lip readers watching television coverage could see Mayor Daley screaming from his seat, "Fuck you, you Jew bastard."

As for the activities outside the convention, Daley made it impossible for the protesters to assemble legally near the convention arena or the delegates' hotels as they marched from their encampments in Lincoln and Grant Parks. In addition, intelligence agents had penetrated their cadres; for example, Jerry Rubin's bodyguard was an undercover Chicago policeman. Some of the government plants acted as agents provocateurs, spurring on the demonstrators to take violent or illegal actions. A minority of the demonstrators did not need the direction of agents provocateurs to provoke and even attack the police. All the same, in several pitched battles seen on television around the world, the police appeared to be the aggressors. "The Whole World is Watching" was the chant, as protesters were clubbed and dragged into paddy wagons in what a government investigative commission later labeled a "police riot." On the last day of the convention, after allegedly seeing objects being thrown from delegates' hotel rooms, the police broke into McCarthy headquarters and beat up scores of innocent campaign workers who were still "keeping clean for Gene."

The melees resulted in 668 arrests. The rest of the battle figures included: one person shot dead, 425 treated for injuries at movement clinics, 200 more treated on the spot, 400 needing treatment for tear-gas inhalation, and 101 treated in hospitals. On the other side, twenty-four car windshields were broken, seventeen police cars were dented or otherwise damaged, 192 of the 11,000 police personnel involved needed hospital treatment; only ten claimed that they were kicked by demonstrators, six said they were hit, and four said they were assaulted by crowds of protesters. No wonder National Security Advisor Walt Rostow thought that the entire nation was "about to become unhinged" that week in August.[5]

Mayor Daley excoriated the media for presenting biased pictures of his calm and responsible police who appeared as heavies in many of the stories of the confrontations. He had little to fear. Despite the chilling images of police beating demonstrators on television and in the print media, a majority of Americans thought that the demonstrators were beating the police and even if the police had used excessive force, "hippies" deserved it. A poll revealed support for the police at 56 to 31 percent while letters to the networks ran 11–1 condemning their alleged biased coverage. These responses revealed the impatience and anger displayed by a majority of Americans against hippie demonstrators and rioters who had filled their television screens and newspapers since the first antiwar demonstrations and urban riots in 1965. They also revealed a growing distaste for the allegedly biased liberal media. Republican candidate Richard Nixon attracted such people with his promise to restore "Law and Order" to his once peaceful nation.

The convention riots and the posture of the Johnson-dominated Democratic Party affected the 1968 campaign in many ways. First, many liberal antiwar activists decided to sit out the election. They denied the party their valuable services handing out leaflets, stuffing envelopes, and ringing doorbells, the sorts of things unpaid campaign workers always did for Democrats. The underfinanced Humphrey campaign sorely missed this assistance, especially since it was contending against the much better financed Republican campaign. Many of those liberals eventually returned to the fold to vote for Humphrey but a significant minority did not, choosing instead not to vote or to opt for third-party candidates such as Black Panther leader Eldridge Cleaver and Benjamin Spock, who were on the ballot in many states. It is interesting to note that when Humphrey, in a speech in San Antonio late in September, finally broke away somewhat from Johnson's position on starting negotiations to end the war, the margin between him and front-runner Nixon began to narrow.

Richard Nixon took the high road on foreign policy during the campaign vowing not to criticize the president's Vietnam policies while negotiations in Paris were entering a delicate stage. He did suggest on many occasions that if elected, he would bring the war to a speedy termination. He never said he had a "secret plan" to end the war, a phrase attributed to him by journalists, but he hinted as much in his vague statements. Off the record, he assured a dovish Republican congressman that he thought he could end the war in six months. Thus, voters who were looking for a peace candidate found little choice between Humphrey and Nixon, both of whom promised to end the war but neither of whom said how.

Moreover, if one was distressed with the turbulence and instability of the Johnson years, Nixon offered the promise of a return to civility and middle-class values and life styles, plus a tough approach to the sort of lawlessness and violent behavior many Americans attributed to the antiwar movement. This promise was not simply conservative red-baiting. In 1967 and 1968, some radicals and would-be revolutionaries had changed their rhetoric and tactics from peaceful protest to civil and uncivil disobedience, and even to revolution. (Third party candidate, former Alabama governor George Wallace, offered voters even tougher policies for dealing with protesters, hippies, radicals, and Communists.)

Vietnam did figure dramatically as an issue during the last week of the campaign in an amazing episode of domestic political espionage that bordered on treason. Prodded by a Soviet Union wary of the old anti-communist Nixon, the North Vietnamese softened their terms for opening formal peace negotiations and the United States responded with a promise of a complete bombing halt. The Republicans were fearful of such an "October Surprise" that might lead those on the fence who wanted to end the war to vote for Humphrey. Nixon's campaign aides sent word to an intermediary to tell the South Vietnamese to reject the Johnson plan for negotiations, promising them that they would receive better terms when Nixon won. They did not need to be urged to reject the arrangement that did not please them.

The president, who had been illegally wiretapping the Nixon campaign and Saigon's embassy in Washington, knew about the Republicans' connection to the South Vietnamese but because he was missing a specific "smoking gun" and did not want to reveal his sources, he remained silent about the affair. When news of the breakthrough in the peace talks reached Americans, Humphrey pulled even with Nixon in the polls. After the South Vietnamese rejection became public, Nixon pulled ahead again and won the election in a squeaker.

Many liberals in the movement were prepared to give Nixon time to end the war. One of his first actions as president-elect was to urge his friends in Saigon to accept the deal that Johnson had arranged before the elections. That action did not impress 8,000 mostly young people who showed up in Washington on January 19, 1969 to hold a counter-inaugural that included a march down Pennsylvania Avenue and a rock n'roll inaugural ball. The next day, they lined the streets jeering at the president, while a minority broke windows, tied up traffic, and engaged in confrontations with the police. In part because of this display, Mobe leaders were more concerned than ever about the increasingly violent fringe elements who appeared at their events. Consequently, they urged their adherents to concentrate their efforts on local activities and not a mass spring demonstration.

With Nixon, the movement faced a more difficult opponent. Unlike Johnson, he was not as concerned about free speech or red-baiting and he did not have to worry about alienating liberals in his party. Under his administration, the legal, illegal, and extralegal intelligence and counter-intelligence operations and the campaigns to harass and persecute radicals organized by the FBI, CIA, NSA, military intelligence, and the White House itself were expanded. The FBI alone assigned 2,000 agents to New Left activity, and the CIA, which is barred from spying operations on U.S. soil, illegally used Operation Chaos to penetrate and watch over domestic peace movements.

The FBI's Cointelpro New Left, which had been set up in 1968, engaged in such illegal activities as publishing newsletters under the names of fictitious organizations that attacked one or another of the left groups or their leaders and sending scurrilous anonymous letters to parents of students who were involved in radical campus groups. The CIA project that became Operation Chaos had been established late in the Johnson administration at the president's request. Between 1967 and 1974, it developed 13,000 files containing information on

300,000 people. For its part, the military recruited R.O.T.C. students to work inside antiwar and antidraft organizations. The IRS helped the counterintelligence effort by agreeing to audit the tax returns of antiwar groups and leaders such as Sidney Peck.

Local agencies were no laggards in this area. For example, Sheli Lukin, who worked for the Chicago Red Squad as an informant, infiltrated eighty-eight organizations over a ten-year period and made it to the national committee of the People's Committee For Peace and Justice in 1972. Irwin Bock, an undercover Chicago police officer, was on the steering committee of the New Mobe in 1969.

Of course, one could argue that considering some radicals' adoption of violent tactics in 1967 and 1968, it was better to overdo the surveillance and even activities that violated the constitutional rights and civil liberties of leftists and liberals in order to protect national security. Between January 1969 and April 1970, there were over 8,000 bombing threats or bombings. Those who resorted to bombings claimed that their aim was not to kill but to disrupt the "System." During the academic year 1969–70, 7,200 young people were arrested on campuses, a number twice that of the previous academic year. Nixon later contended that since the president alone is the ultimate authority on what constitutes a threat to national security, he can do whatever is necessary to protect the nation. He came close to saying that even actions that appeared illegal on the surface could be justified when they were taken to protect national security. After his illegal and extralegal intelligence programs were revealed during the Watergate hearings in 1973 and 1974 and again in 1975, during hearings on illegal practices of American intelligence agencies, most observers viewed Nixon's tactics as a dangerous threat to the Constitution.

Nixon believed that "many leaders of the antiwar movement were hard-core militants of the New Left who hated the United States" and that young people who opposed the war did so not because of "moral conviction" but "to keep from getting their asses shot off." In addition, their activities gave "encouragement to the enemy" that "prolonged the war."[6] Like Johnson he was convinced that Communists abroad lay behind the actions adopted by American antiwar leaders. And like Johnson, he was disappointed when the CIA and FBI could not produce the evidence to support his suspicions. He contemplated setting up a new intelligence agency in the White House, as envisaged in the aborted Huston Plan, in part because he believed that the existing agencies were not doing an adequate job uncovering subversives in the movement. Nixon later contended that the antiwar movement helped rally Americans to his foreign policy because the "demonstrations . . . polarized the debate and left me with more support for the war than I otherwise would have." They "hurt their cause" because they "were very violent."[7]

Despite his claim that the movement had little effect on him, Nixon monitored its activities closely and, like Johnson, discovered that protesters were able to constrain the movements of the president of the United States. When informed that students at Ohio State University, where he was scheduled to give a speech in June 1969, were planning a large demonstration, he canceled the engagement, saving face by concocting an emergency trip to Midway Island to meet South Vietnamese president Nguyen Van Thieu.

Although his was a Republican administration, as during the Johnson years, many of the children and wives of aides and cabinet officials opposed the war. Included in that group were children of chief of staff H. R. Haldeman, domestic policy adviser John Ehrlichman, Secretary of Defense Melvin Laird, Secretary of Labor George Shultz, and even, allegedly, a young daughter of Vice President Spiro Agnew. (To irritate Nixon and Agnew, Abbie Hoffman announced to the press that he had had sexual relations with the thirteen-year-old girl.) Several of National Security Advisor Henry Kissinger's aides sometimes saw their antiwar wives marching by the White House on their way to a demonstration.

AS THE NEW NIXON ADMINISTRATION WAS GETTING ITS OWN HOUSE IN order, the movement was in a period of transition. Many leaders and activists were becoming frustrated and burned out from their failure to stop the war, despite enormous energies expended, and from the constant enervating and often vicious political infighting among the sectarian groups that ran the coalitions. It was not coincidental that 1969 was the year during which Benjamin Spock had to be hospitalized with heartbeat problems while his forty-year marriage came apart. Similarly, indefatigable antiwarrior Sidney Peck and his wife found it necessary to seek emergency therapy to save their marriage that same year.

But the movement was still a potential threat to Nixon, and if anything, seemed to have greater potential to influence opinion now that its allies included more Democratic officials who no longer had to worry about losing patronage or party support because they angered the president. The new president had to demonstrate to the Communists, not only the Vietnamese Communists but the Soviet and Chinese ones as well, that mobs in the street would have no influence on his policy. He soon established a diplomatic system that he hoped would compare in efficiency to those of dictatorial systems. Based in the White House under Kissinger and not in the State Department under Secretary of State William Rogers, the new undemocratic system was established primarily to keep its policies secret from members of the diplomatic establishment, including State Department officials, and the Joint Chiefs of Staff, who might leak administration secrets to the media or to Congress. In fact, the chiefs had to engage in an unprecedented domestic espionage project in which their agent in the White House pilfered thousands of documents from the National Security Council so they would know what was going on in U.S. foreign policy. Nixon's obsession with secrecy was one way to keep the crowds in the street uninformed about his machinations, which certainly would have displeased them.

In one such machination in March, he authorized the bombing of Cambodia, an initiative kept secret from most members of the government, the media, the public, and, especially, the antiwar movement— but not from the Communists in Southeast Asia. Aside from the strategic importance of bombing Cambodian segments of the Ho Chi Minh Trail system through which Hanoi transported materiel and troops to the war in the south, Nixon sent a message to the North Vietnamese that he could get away with such bold actions without Americans discovering them. When a story about the bombing appeared in the *New York Times* in May, the White House launched an illegal wiretapping project to discover who had leaked the information. Nixon's investigators did not discover the culprit but fortunately for him, after an initial flurry of interest, the story faded away without a follow-up. The precedent of going after leakers through illegal means directed by the White House led to the establishment of the "Plumbers," whose activities became part of the bill of particulars in the impeachment of the president. This secret bombing would not be the only time that Cambodia played a significant role in the relationship between the antiwar movement and the president.

DURING HIS EARLY MONTHS IN OFFICE, NIXON FACED A SMATTERING of movement activities that had become a normal part of an administration's life by 1969. In early February, 1,000 members of CALC (it had shortened its name from CALCAV) came to Washington to demonstrate and lobby. Several even obtained an audience with Kissinger, a German-Jewish American, who blanched when Rabbi Heschel asked, "Don't you think that if we keep doing this, America will look more and more like Nazi Germany."[8] Late in February, active-duty soldiers at Fort Jackson, South Carolina organized a group called GI's United Against the War in Vietnam, the next month protesters vandalized Dow Chemical's headquarters in Washington, and in April at Harvard, rioting led to 196 arrests, with 48 people needing medical attention, and a ten-day strike.

Few noticed at the time the founding in March of the Committee of Concerned Asian Scholars. By 1969 the vast majority of specialists on Asia and Indochina on American campuses opposed the war. Some of the older scholars, who had for years been involved in government projects, still supported the administration. But almost all the younger scholars and graduate students in Asian centers such as those at Berkeley, Cornell, Harvard, Wisconsin, and Michigan were against the war. They soon began publishing analyses, informed by the latest scholarship, in their *Bulletin of Concerned Asian Scholars*. In many other academic disciplines in the late '60s, radical caucuses developed, calling on their apolitical associations to take a stand against injustice at home and violence abroad.

The major antiwar events of spring 1969 were the fifth annual mass demonstrations—this time on Easter weekend, April 5 and 6. With the Mobe refusing for tactical reasons to organize them, a new organization, the National Action Group (NAG), stepped into the breach with "Resistance and Renewal" protests. Dominated by pacifists from the AFSC, WRL, and CNVA, its leadership also included representatives from SANE, WILPF, and the SCLC. The Student Mobe organized campus events. Over 150,000 protesters turned out in more than forty cities, with as many as 50,000 in New York's Central Park and 30,000 in Chicago. The crowds in Chicago, Atlanta, and Austin broke records that weekend, while the 150,000 total made Resistance and Renewal the second largest protest to date. As part of the activities, on Easter Sunday, four young men were "crucified" on large crosses in front of the White House.

Untold numbers of other doves may have been nervous about participating that weekend because, on March 29, the Justice Department had indicted eight activists on charges of conspiracy and traveling across state lines to "incite a riot" in Chicago the previous August. The eight included Chicago demonstration leaders Dellinger, Davis, and Hayden as well as Yippie co-conspirators, Hoffman and Rubin. The long-haired Hoffman received a prison haircut courtesy of the sheriff of Cook County, who was the brother of Nixon's long-time personal secretary, Rose Mary Woods.

The Justice Department would have found it difficult to bring charges against the organizers of the Easter demonstrations. Most of the off-campus activities, which were led by adults, were peaceful. Silent vigils, guerrilla theater, and prayer services shared the stage with demonstrations and rallies on this occasion, which often featured a sprinkling of uniformed Vietnam veterans who had begun to appear prominently at such activities. The media took comparatively little interest in the events, which had become so routine that they were no longer considered newsworthy, unless of course many people were arrested or ended up in the hospital. Even the *Guardian,* a left-wing weekly, noted the "incredible boredom of ritual parade." The *New York Times* headlined a story adjacent to the demonstration story, "Nixon Has Begun to End the War in Vietnam"[9]

In the early days of his administration, Nixon established a White House office to prepare the most elaborate daily media surveys ever sent to the Oval Office. He was acutely aware of the importance of the media in affecting opinion and especially concerned about what he contended was the major electronic and print institutions' (NBC, CBS, ABC, *Time, Newsweek, The New York Times,* and *Washington Post*) bias against him. As for the media in general, he thought at most only 35 percent of newspapers and magazines could be considered fair. All the same, he did better on Easter Weekend than could have been expected. On that occasion, his media monitors accurately reported the relative lack of interest in the demonstrations exhibited by even liberal publications hostile to the administration and its Vietnam policy.

The antiwar movement had to come up with something new. In the early spring, Sam Brown and David Hawk, two young liberals who had worked on the McCarthy campaign, developed a "Declaration of Conscience," which was signed by 253 campus student-body presidents and student-newspaper editors. In their declaration, they declared the war "immoral and unjust" and vowed not to "serve in the military as long as the war in Vietnam continues."[10] On April 29, a delegation from the group, including National Student Association staffer Hawk, met with Kissinger and Ehrlichman who were unable to promise them a speedy end to the war, counseling instead that they be patient. Of their "Declaration of Conscience," the national security advisor commented that he did not think the war in Vietnam was of the "greatest moral magnitude" to justify conscientious objection.[11]

Those attending the meeting concluded, "These guys are going to be worse than the last bunch."[12] The antiwar movement had to get moving again with something new. Thus it was that Hawk and Brown, along with several of their colleagues, came up with the most effective and original protest idea of the entire period, the Moratorium. Instead of mass demonstrations in two cities (New York or Washington and San Francisco) on a fall weekend, the Moratorium would be a decentralized event that would take place in cities all over the United States during a weekday, Wednesday, October 15, 1969. On that day, people would participate in a moratorium from work or school for anywhere from a few minutes to several hours to register their opposition to the continuation of the war at rallies, marches, vigils, prayer sessions, or by leafleting and participating in whatever activities local moratorium committees organized. Further, the Moratorium promised that if the war was still going on in November, it would sponsor a two-day event, with a three-day event planned for December and so on.

Although the national Moratorium committee established general guidelines, this operation was decentralized. For that reason, it was also cheaper to manage than previous coalitions that had to organize mass demonstrations. Finally, by moving the demonstrations from a few large cities to hundreds of smaller venues, Moratorium leaders were also moving them away from the few places where sizable contingents of unruly radicals performed their own antiwar actions.

Brown and Hawk made their appeal to liberals and moderates. Looking back on the era, Brown noted the disjunction between much of the leadership of the movement and those who showed up for demonstrations. "Virtually all the antiwar leadership," he wrote, "was of the 'inevitability by-product school,'" which saw a crisis in capitalism as the cause of American involvement in Vietnam, "while most of the participants in marches and campaigns were of the 'aberrational-occurrence school'" in which the democratic nation made a singular blunder in Southeast Asia.[13]

Not to be outdone, former Mobe leaders, generally to the left of those of the Moratorium, met in July in Cleveland to reconstitute themselves as the New Mobilization Committee to End the War in Vietnam. They began planning a mass demonstration for Washington in November. In addition, New Mobe members sometimes began to take the lead in organizing Moratorium activities in their communities. SDS, the organization that sponsored the first such demonstration in 1965 and whose officers such as Tom Hayden participated in later antiwar actions, broke into several radical pieces at its June convention and, after a paroxysm of violence, all but disappeared as a nationwide organization in 1970.

By the time that the Moratorium and the New Mobe had set the date for their fall activities, Nixon's plans for Vietnam also became clearer. He embarked on a policy of "Vietnamization," in which he would build up the Saigon government's armed forces so that they could assume more of the ground combat tasks from the Americans who would be slowly withdrawn. He was convinced that such a policy would lessen the pressure he faced at home from young people and their parents who were concerned about American casualties. Nixon announced his first withdrawal of 25,000 troops in June at a meeting on Midway Island with South Vietnamese president Thieu, where he also announced what would later be called the Nixon Doctrine, a policy that in effect said, no more Vietnams.

Doves were not impressed with Vietnamization and Nixon's promise to pull out so few of the almost 540,000 troops in Vietnam that summer. At that rate, the war could go on for several more years. President Thieu was even less pleased with Vietnamization because at a certain point, he would be left alone to fight the North Vietnamese and the Vietcong. Further, if Hanoi knew that the United States was going to pull out all of its troops in the future, what inducement did it have to negotiate while they were still there?

Nixon gave them an "inducement." Aside from the bombing of Cambodia and the increase in the bombing of North Vietnam under loopholes in the previous year's agreement to open peace talks, the president issued a secret ultimatum in July to North Vietnam—soften your negotiating positions by November 1 or face an unspecified military escalation. His advisers then began working on Operation Duck Hook, feasibility studies of military escalation that would be a "savage blow" of some sort. The November 1 deadline fell two weeks after the date of the Moratorium and two weeks before the date of the New Mobe's demonstration in Washington. Movement leaders, of course, knew nothing about the ultimatum.

As the deadline neared, Nixon was more concerned about trouble with Congress than with doves in the streets. Throughout his administration, the Democratic-controlled Congress introduced scores of resolutions meant to tie his hands in Vietnam. Although it was not approved, the Goodell Resolution of September 25, 1969, which called for U.S. withdrawal from Vietnam by December 1970, was characteristic. Such a resolution, Nixon reasoned, could only encourage the Communists as they contemplated their responses to his ultimatum. He was not pleased with Senator Charles Goodell, a Republican from New York, whom the administration helped defeat in the 1970 elections.

Nixon soon discovered that the Moratorium caused him more immediate problems than Goodell's failed resolution. In two moves timed to affect public opinion, he announced another troop withdrawal of 35,000 on September 16, and four days later, the replacement of the unpopular General Lewis Hershey, the head of Selective Service, a move he hoped would cool anti-draft fever on the campuses. The measures did not help at Harvard where on October 7, its faculty endorsed the Moratorium by a 391–16 tally.

Using another tack against the protest, Nixon asserted on September 26, "Under no circumstances will I be affected whatever by it" and, on the eve of the Moratorium, explained further, "To allow government policy to be made in the streets would destroy the democratic procedure. It would give the decision not to the majority . . . but to those with the loudest voices."[14]

Spiro Agnew was busy on September 26 as well. The feisty vice president, who was Nixon's Nixon on the hustings, launched a campaign against the liberal media ("a small and unelected elite"[15]) hoping to intimidate the networks in particular against covering the Moratorium live. He may have been successful in helping to convince broadcasters to limit their coverage to videotape.

The administration also encouraged the American Legion in its campaign to urge Americans to fly the flag on October 15 as a sign of opposition to the demonstrations. The flag, which administration aides began wearing in their lapels, soon became a prominent symbol of support for President Nixon. Other groups called for patriotic Americans on October 15 to drive with their lights on as another reflection of opposition to doves. Finally, employers threatened to fire or otherwise punish employees who left work to join Moratorium activities that Wednesday. In several instances, they followed through on those threats.

Nixon and Agnew had good reason to fear the Moratorium. The novel concept struck the right chord among much of the population. The first of three advertisements in the *New York Times* announcing the program for October 15 and, especially, soliciting money, was the most successful ad of its kind to date. The Moratorium was soon endorsed by at least nine members of Congress and W. Averell Harriman, Johnson's chief negotiator in Paris in 1968, along with a host of moderates and liberals who heretofore had steered clear of antiwar demonstrations. As many as two million people in over two hundred cities and towns participated in Moratorium activities. Participants ranged from at least 15 combat soldiers in Vietnam wearing black armbands, to 100,000 listening on the Boston Common to South Dakota senator George McGovern and setting a record for the largest political crowd in that city's history, to 250,000 in New York who attended rallies in Bryant Park and on Wall Street. Many Broadway shows canceled their matinees that afternoon and Republican mayor John Lindsay ordered flags to be flown at half mast on municipal buildings. As many as 90 percent of high school students in New York failed to show up for class that Wednesday.

Turnouts were impressive as well in Chicago, Washington, Minneapolis, Salt Lake City, and Pittsburgh, where the city council endorsed the demonstration. Even more impressive were the dignified silent vigils and prayer meetings held in several hundred small towns where antiwar demonstrations had not been very popular. Most important, the vast majority of participants everywhere were adults, often in coats and ties, skirts and heels, who shunned obscene chants and radical placards to tell their government, quite simply, that they were dissatisfied with the pace that had been established for ending U.S. military involvement in Southeast Asia. Only a week earlier, several hundred members of the nihilistic Weatherman faction of the fast-fading SDS had taken to the streets to destroy property and combat the police in "Days of Rage" in Chicago. One would have thought that fear of comparable violence from militants on the fringe would have kept many of the moderate doves in their homes on October 15.

There was some violence, especially in Washington, which hurt the predominantly peaceful image of the Moratorium. Even more hurtful were the public greetings that North Vietnamese leader Pham Van Dong (Ho Chi Minh died in September) sent to the Moratorium. One would have thought that by then, he would have realized that such greetings may have thrilled the handful of revolutionaries in the crowd, but most antiwar protesters were disturbed when he tainted their activities with a red tinge. Each time this happened, administration supporters used it to denounce the demonstrators.

The television networks loved the Moratorium. It provided them with scores of colorful and touching vignettes, from coast to coast, with an occasional counterdemonstration thrown in for balance. ABC devoted almost its entire evening newscast to the event. NBC began its broadcast with an unprecedented nine-minute montage of pictures and sound without a word of narration from the anchor. The three networks all began with stories from the East Coast and then moved across the nation ending up in California revealing that the Moratorium was observed most everywhere, except, by and large, in the South. No other antiwar activity either before or after the October 15 Moratorium was treated so generously and favorably by the networks.

The same held true in the major print media. *Time,* after commenting on the scope and quality of the protests ("a sedate Woodstock Festival of Peace"), noted, "Nixon cannot escape the effects of the antiwar movement." On the eve of the Moratorium, *Newsweek* headlined a story, "Nixon in Trouble," and after the event remarked, "There had never been a phenomenon quite like it."[16] According to *Life* magazine, it was a phenomenon "without parallel, the largest expression of public dissent ever seen in this country."[17]

Contrary to his previously declared indifference to the Moratorium, Nixon did pay attention to its many manifestations and carefully examined his media monitors' accounts. Although they tended to emphasize the minority of negative comments in the press and although polls in the weeks after the demonstrations revealed that the president still had the support of a majority of Americans, the administration was rattled by the most impressive antiwar demonstration in the nation's history. What impressed them was the very favorable coverage in the media and the related fact that so many middle-class adults, together with prominent liberal and moderate officials and opinion leaders, participated in the dignified, respectful, and unique events.

The Moratorium affected Nixon's decision not to call Hanoi's bluff after it failed to meet his ultimatum by November 1. It is true that those who planned Duck Hook could not come up with a foolproof program of military escalation that would cripple the North Vietnamese war effort sufficiently to alter their diplomatic posture without challenging the Russians and Chinese to intervene militarily to aid their ally. They also realized that any major change in American tactics would upset a good portion of the population that supported the president because they believed he was deescalating. Such an action would obviously have outraged the antiwar movement and its supporters in the media. Nixon blamed the Moratorium for his inability to act against Hanoi after the November 1 deadline passed. The Moratorium "had undercut the credibility of the ultimatum" because it encouraged the North Vietnamese, he asserted, and thus it "destroyed whatever small possibility may still have existed to end the war."[18] Here, Nixon may have been using the Moratorium as a convenient excuse to explain his failure to act the tough guy on November 1.

Antiwar leaders never knew about their "victory" because Nixon's July ultimatum was a secret. But they did know that he was worried about them as he and Agnew launched an accelerated attack against the movement and the media over the several weeks following the protests. The administration was noticeably concerned about the second Moratorium, called for November 13 and 14 and the New Mobe's mass demonstration in Washington on November 15. If they were anything like the October 15 events, the administration would take another beating in the media, and perhaps, among the public as well.

In the days after the Moratorium, Nixon began working on what he would later label the most important speech of his presidency. Behind that speech was his vow that he "was not going to be pushed around by the demonstrators and rabble in the streets."[19] His celebrated "Silent Majority" speech, delivered on television on November 3, outlined his policy of peace with honor and a slow but steady withdrawal of American forces as Vietnamization took hold. Most important, he appealed to the "great silent majority" of Americans who approved his policy but were not the sort of people to demonstrate publicly or to speak up because, "North Vietnam cannot humiliate the United States. Only Americans can do that."[20]

The president was elated with the response to his speech. After two days, over 130,000 letters and telegrams had been received at the White

House, with the president's position favored by a 10-to-1 ratio. Few Americans knew that thousands of those letters had been generated by Republican operatives in a well-organized White House campaign to make headlines by fabricating favorable responses to Nixon's initiatives. All the same, the polls did reveal that a silent majority supported the president, especially when he asked it to choose between him and the "effete corps of impudent snobs" villified by Vice President Agnew on October 19.[21]

Nixon was not as happy with the media's response to his speech. Consequently, with an eye to the upcoming demonstrations, he stepped up his attack on the press, again unleashing Spiro Agnew to carry the fight on this front. On November 13, the vice president told a Des Moines audience about a small group of liberals in New York and Washington who dominated the flow of opinion in the United States. As with the Silent Majority speech, the response to Agnew's attack was popular. Tens of thousands of letters poured into the networks favoring his position by 2 or 3 to 1. In addition, Nixon had asked the Republican chair of the Federal Communications Commission to investigate the biases he thought he saw in the networks' post Silent Majority Speech "instant analyses." Striking a populist tone, he contended that the American people did not need the networks to explain to them what the president said. Television was more vulnerable to intimidation than print media since stations were federally licensed.

They were intimidated. The Moratorium on November 13 and 14, and the Mobilization in Washington and San Francisco on November 15, the largest ever peace demonstrations in those cities, received no live coverage, and more important, received far less attention on newscasts than the Moratorium the previous month. Convinced that the doves were having a negative effect on his attempts to bring the war in Vietnam to a successful conclusion, Nixon had declared all-out war on the movement and its supporters in the media. Only by rallying his majority would he be able to pursue the sorts of tough military policies that he thought would bring peace with honor.

On top of the Silent Majority speech and the offensive against the media, the administration took the line that radicals bent on tearing up the capital controlled the demonstrations. This suggestion was nonsense, but there were a handful of "crazies" on the fringes of the Mobilization who planned to emulate their role models, the Weathermen, who themselves demanded a bribe of $20,000 from the organizers to stay away from the demonstration. They did not receive their money. More nefarious was the FBI's scheme to demand $25,000 from the Mobe for the fictitious "Black United Front of the District of Columbia." The agency hoped to create "bickering, resentment, and distrust," among the leaders of the peace coalition through this ploy.[22] Further, after October's Moratorium, Attorney General John Mitchell approved a new request by J. Edgar Hoover to wiretap movement organizations to improve the administration's intelligence gathering. By predicting violence and also making it difficult for organizers to obtain parade permits, the administration hoped to keep the crowds down.

Considering the forces arrayed against them, the Moratorium and Mobilization did quite well with impressive and imaginative demonstrations that generated large crowds. On November 13, the Moratorium held a March Against Death in which, over a two-day period, 40,000 demonstrators, each carrying a placard with the name of a GI killed in Vietnam, marched from Arlington to the White House where they called out the name on their placard, and then marched on to the Capitol where they deposited the placard in coffins. In a side event, 186 demonstrators, led by Jane Hart, the wife of Michigan Democratic senator Phil Hart, were arrested after trying to hold a Mass on the steps of the Pentagon.

In an action on Friday, November 14 unrelated to the official events, as many as 10,000 militants staged several demonstrations outside the embassy of South Vietnam, while several hundred people turned in their draft cards at the Justice Department. In one of the actions outside the embassy, police had to use tear gas to turn away a small number of people who threatened to storm the building. These activities received a good deal of media play, much to the disgust of the Moratorium and Mobe leaders who took pride in how peaceful their events had been.

On that same Friday, scores of communities held Moratorium actions similar to, but nowhere as numerous or mediagenic as, those of October 15. The most interesting may have been in New York's Central Park where demonstrators fell to the ground, simulating being killed in action, while black and white balloons were released, symbolizing those already killed and those who would soon be killed, as "Taps" was played.

On Saturday, it was the New Mobe's turn. Well over 250,000 doves were attracted to its Washington demonstration and over 100,000 to its rally in Golden Gate Park in San Francisco. In Washington, they were first met at the assembly point on the Mall by Senator Eugene McCarthy, who encouraged them as they set off down Pennsylvania Avenue to the Washington Monument. Marching under a banner, "Silent Majority for Peace," they carried twelve coffins containing placards from the March Against Death. Marshals from the Mobe were able to maintain discipline, even when confronted by militants who urged marchers to join them in attacking targets away from the parade route. At the monument, Senators McGovern and Goodell and comedian-activist Dick Gregory were among the speakers. The Mobe rejected Abbie Hoffman's and Jerry Rubin's request to speak. Much of the crowd was more interested in the all-star entertainment from four casts of the musical "Hair," John Denver, Pete Seeger, Arlo Guthrie, Leonard Bernstein, and Mitch Miller, who led a singalong of "Give Peace a Chance" that lasted ten minutes.

Generally, at such demonstrations, serious political talks, which were not always easy to hear, were interspersed with the music that blasted over the entire crowd. Cynical observers were correct in noting that a good number of the "demonstrators" were attracted to the music more than the by-now-familiar harangues from the politicos. If the weather was nice, what could be more pleasant on a weekend than to sit on a blanket with friends, drinking wine and perhaps smoking marijuana, listening to the free concert provided by the organizers of the "peace festival?" These events were social as well as political, with one young member of Nixon's Security Council admitting that he sneaked out of the White House to attend them in order to pick up girls.

At the end of the rally, David Dellinger took the microphone, as he had done in Washington on October 21, 1967, to invite people to join him in a march to the Justice Department for a rally. He was joined by 10,000 radicals and militant pacifists, some of whom carried Vietcong flags and pictures of Communist icons. The rally ended up in a violent confrontation with the police—"Off the pigs," they shouted—with a good deal of broken storefront windows, looting, and arrests.

Although the demonstrations of November 13–15 were among the most impressive of the war, Nixon won this round with the antiwar movement. The media overemphasized the violent aspects of the events, which were not sanctioned by the organizers and involved only relative handfuls of militants. Moreover, the television networks, especially, did not devote the sort of space to the demonstrations that they had the previous month, because of administration pressure. *Newsweek* headlined its story, "The Big March: On a Treadmill?" concluding that the antiwar movement had no place to go, pressured from the Right by the administration and from the Left by the militants. The Left pressure exerted itself at the New Mobe's December meeting when, in part because of the mixed reviews of their mammoth Washington demonstration, moderates were elbowed aside by radicals. Even more important, the Moratorium, which promised monthly demonstrations, never came close to replicating the turnouts for the October and November events. In December its leaders gave up the idea of regular monthly protests.

Some journalists noted that the fervor was fading from the November demonstrators who seemed to show up as a matter of routine. In addition, Nixon supporters held rallies during the same period in places like Pittsburgh, Birmingham, and Chicago that drew relatively impressive crowds. Antiwarriors were frustrated once again. Although Nixon had reduced the number of American troops in Vietnam from 540,000 in January 1969, to 475,000 by year's end, with the promise of further reductions to come, the war continued and the casualties, especially for the Vietnamese, continued to mount. What more could they do?

AS HE LOOKED OVER THE LESS-THAN-POSITIVE COVERAGE OF THE movement, the polls that showed only 21 percent for immediate withdrawal, and the visible manifestations of support from the Silent Majority, the president had good reason to believe that the twin campaigns, his launched on November 3 and Spiro Agnew's on November 13, had been successful. He was confident that he was well on the way toward building a base of support that would permit him a freer hand to exercise military power to bring the war to a successful end, which for him meant the survival of a non-Communist entity in South Vietnam.

NOTES

1. Wells, *The War Within*, 265.
2. Klein, ed., *Dissent, Power, and Confrontation*, 140.
3. Hayden, *Reunion*, 262.
4. Wells, *The War Within*, 237.

5. Ibid., 280.

6. Melvin Small, *The Presidency of Richard Nixon* (Lawrence: University Press of Kansas, 1999), 69.

7. Monica Crowley, *Nixon Off the Record: His Candid Commentary on People and Politics* (New York: Random House, 1966), 257, 258.

8. Wells, *The War Within*, 292.

9. Small, *Covering Dissent*, 91.

10. Zaroulis and Sullivan, *Who Spoke Up?* 245.

11. Ibid., 245.

12. Wells, *The War Within*, 294.

13. Sam Brown, "The Defeat of the Antiwar Movement," in *The Vietnam Legacy*, ed., Anthony Lake (New York: New York University Press, 1976), 123.

14. Small, *The Presidency of Richard Nixon*, 74.

15. Anderson, *The Movement*, 331.

16. Small, *Covering Dissent*, 101, 102.

17. Fred Halstead, *Out Now: A Participant's Account of the Movement in the U.S. against the Vietnam War* (New York: Pathfinder, 1978), 488.

18. Small, *The Presidency of Richard Nixon*, 74.

19. Small, *Johnson, Nixon, and the Doves*, 188.

20. Ibid., 189.

21. Robert Mann, *A Grand Delusion: America's Descent into Vietnam* (New York: Basic Books, 2001), 642.

22. Zaroulis and Sullivan, *Who Spoke Up?* 276.

CHAPTER Seven

HALTING ESCALATION

THE ANTIWAR MOVEMENT PEAKED IN THE FALL OF 1969. FROM that point on, despite an impressive series of demonstrations in May 1970 and in April 1971, it became less cohesive and more fragmented than it had ever been before. And, of course, it had never been a very cohesive movement. The conflict between sectarian political groups expanded as did the general conflict between the small minority of violent revolutionaries and nihilists and the rest of the movement. Further, Nixon ordered an increase in the intensity of surveillance and harassment programs from the FBI, CIA, IRS, and the White House itself that helped to weaken and contain the doves as well as his perceived enemies in the media.

The president promised in 1968 to "Bring Us Together." Beginning with the Silent Majority speech a little more than a year later, he helped create a polarized nation with a majority that opposed violence, instability, and the counterculture confronting an increasingly isolated minority of liberals and radicals. For many Americans, it was difficult to distinguish between the noisy protesters in the streets and the Weathermen who made headlines in early March 1970 when three of its group were killed in the "bomb factory" they maintained in a Greenwich Village townhouse. At the time, the Weathermen could claim only 300 active members.

Nixon speechwriter William Safire pointed out that the movement was "useful as the villain, the object against which all our supporters could be rallied."[1] On the other side of the fence, Tom Hayden thought that the nation under Nixon was heading toward "civil war."[2] The president helped his cause with Vietnamization, which accelerated in 1970 as an increasing number of Americans came home from the front. On December 15, 1969, for example, he announced his intention to bring home soon another 50,000 boys. It also helped that his draft lottery system began operating in January 1970. To some degree, it eased the concerns of young men and their families about the previous system of random call-ups.

There was also a problem of burn-out. Hundreds of thousands of people had been involved exhaustively with the antiwar movement since 1965. Many, particularly those not bound by a lifelong commitment to one or another formal political movement, had decided that it was time to get on with their lives. This change became more and more the case for college students in the early '70s as the economic outlook dimmed, in part because of the cost of the war. In 1965, armed with their fresh BA's, they had little trouble finding good jobs in the then thriving economy. That prospect became less of a certainty during Nixon's first term, suggesting another reason why some students left the pavements for their studies.

All the same, Nixon did not have a free hand to escalate in pursuit of victory in Vietnam. Most Americans accepted his policy of gradual withdrawal from the battlefield with the end of the war, if not in sight, at least likely in the near future. Indeed, that expectation was another reason for the decline of the movement. However, any deviation from that policy would rekindle the movement and arouse the general population. Such was the case in the spring of 1970.

THE TWO MAJOR PEACE COALITIONS, THE MORATORIUM AND THE Mobilization, were still in operation in early 1970. The Moratorium project of longer protests each month had fizzled the previous December and its poorly organized "Peace Action Days" of January through March attracted few participants and virtually no significant media coverage. CALC's call for a seventy-day partial fast from Lent through Passover also failed to attract much attention. More innovative but of dubious legality was the bill that passed the Massachusetts legislature in April that prohibited the dispatch of young men from its state to combat zones for more than sixty days unless Congress declared war.

Despite the dismal prospects for a major spring demonstration, the Mobilization, the Moratorium, and the Student Mobe called for nationwide actions from April 13 through April 18 with April 15, or "tax day," chosen for the most massive mobilizations. Antiwar cadres could still bring out their troops with over 75,000 in Boston, 40,000 in New York, 25,000 in Chicago, and 20,000 in San Francisco. But militants broke up the New York demonstration and rioters caused damage to stores around Harvard and in Berkeley, and those actions dominated the headlines on April 16, much to the administration's pleasure. Moreover, movement stories had been pushed from the front pages by the drama of the life-threatening dangers encountered by astronauts aboard *Apollo 13* on their mission to the moon from April 11 to April 17. On April 21, the Moratorium committee disbanded, in part because of its inability to produce large demonstrations that were not disrupted by radicals.

President Nixon was heartened by the success of his campaign to win the hearts and minds of the American people, an accomplishment that had begun with the Silent Majority Speech the previous November. Polls revealed that a majority of the population supported his policy of gradual demobilization of the U.S. military in Vietnam and the turnout for, and coverage of, the spring protests demonstrated that the movement was in decline. These factors contributed to his decision during the last weeks of April to send American and South Vietnamese troops into Cambodia. He was also getting back at the North Vietnamese, who had called his bluff the previous November when they made no concessions in face of his threats of escalation. In addition, he was challenging a Democratic Senate that had just rejected the second of two successive Supreme Court appointments.

For years the military brass had advocated the invasion of Cambodia to stem the flow of supplies and men from North Vietnam into South Vietnam along the Ho Chi Minh Trail system in Cambodia. Cambodia was a nominally neutral country whose eastern border areas had long been occupied by the North Vietnamese. As we have seen, beginning in March 1969, Nixon had ordered the secret bombing of those areas. Now, confident that he had most of his nation behind him, he announced the invasion of Cambodia on nationwide television on April 30. He did not quite announce an "invasion"—he called it an "incursion," which sounded more temporary and less of an escalation than an invasion. He explained that he was also going to destroy COSVN, the Communists' Cambodian headquarters for the direction of the war in South Vietnam. He made the escalation part of his program of Vietnamization. By weakening the North Vietnamese ability to make war, he informed the nation, it would buy more time for the South Vietnamese to develop their own defense capabilities.

After hearing this rationale for what seemed like an escalation, Secretary of State William Rogers allegedly commented, "This will make the students puke."[3] Nixon expected his action would lead to widespread protests from the then virtually moribund antiwar movement but he was confident that he could handle them. In fact, he almost looked forward to the combat. "We'll catch unshirted hell no matter what we do," he told one of his aides, "so we'd better get on with it."[4]

Nixon's speech was a complete surprise to everyone except for an inner circle in the White House. After all, only ten days earlier, he had announced a massive 150,000 troop withdrawal. And now he was escalating. Campuses erupted as they had never done before as hundreds of thousands of students poured into their quads after the address demanding a response from antiwar leaders. He made matters far worse when he was quoted the next day suggesting that protesters were merely "bums blowing up the campus." It turns out that he was referring to the April 24 bombing of the Center for Advanced Study of the Behavioral Sciences adjacent to Stanford University, which, at the time, was experiencing a series of rowdy demonstrations. That still unsolved bombing resulted in the destruction of a good portion of the life's work of Indian sociologist, M. N. Srinivas and came close to destroying the only manuscript copy of Harvard philosopher John Rawls's then-unpublished magisterial, *A Theory of Justice*.

Nixon might have been able to weather the initial storm were it not for the killings at Kent State University. In the wake of his April 30 address, Kent State experienced a series of violent reactions, including the burning of a ROTC building, which led the governor to call out the National Guard. On May 4, during a peaceful if rhetorically provocative demonstration in the middle of the campus, jittery and untrained guardsmen, claiming they had been the targets of stones, fired live ammunition into the crowd, some of whom were demonstrators, others who were students going to class. Guardsmen killed four and wounded nine. Apparently the firing began spontaneously—no one has ever claimed to have given or to have heard an order to fire. A hasty, insensitive press release from the administration concerning the killings only made things worse. The White House announced, "This should remind us all once again that when dissent turns to violence, it invites tragedy."[5]

The eruptions at universities throughout the nation following the Kent State tragedy were unprecedented in American history. Student activists immediately called for a nationwide strike. Two days after the killings, over eighty college presidents had closed their institutions for anywhere from one day to the end of the semester. Governor Ronald Reagan temporarily closed the entire University of California system to prevent more violence. Between May 4 and May 8, there were an average of 100 campus demonstrations a day. At the end of a week after the Kent State killings, over 150 colleges had experienced successful student strikes. During that same period, more than 100 colleges reported significant violent acts on their campuses. In the end, at least 448 colleges experienced strikes or closures during the first two weeks in May, 89 percent of private and 76 percent of public universities had experienced some form of protest on campus, and governors called out the National Guard to keep order on at least 24 occasions. Craig McNamara, the son of the former Defense Secretary, participated in one especially destructive rampage on the Stanford campus.

Agitation occurred not only on college campuses. One activist wrote of New York City, "It was something I'd never seen before and never seen since. . . . I could feel the polarization. . . . On that day or two after the Cambodian invasion, this whole city was filled with thousands of people all over the street debating."[6]

It was not all serious politics in some venues. At Southern Illinois University, one happy student described the closing of his institution, "We had a huge party. People were running through the streets naked," while another remembered that "People were smoking dope on the street. . . . It was a circus atmosphere. It was a lot of fun."[7]

Much of this unrest took place before May 14, when two were killed and twelve were wounded after police fired on students at Jackson State College, a predominantly Black institution in Mississippi. By that time, the crisis situation on college campuses had begun to wind down. Nonetheless, the relative lack of response to the Jackson State killings of Black students stood in stark contrast to the reaction that followed the killings of White students at Kent State.

The president also confronted widespread criticism from within his administration. Three members of Kissinger's National Security Council staff resigned, including Anthony Lake, who two decades later became Bill Clinton's first national security advisor. Commissioner of Education James Allen and Secretary of Interior Walter Hickel disagreed publicly with the invasion and 250 foreign-service officers sent a note of protest to Rogers. The latter action enraged the president who called the undersecretary of state, demanding "I want you to make sure all those sons of bitches are fired first thing in the morning."[8] Nixon himself later recalled this period as "among the darkest" during his tenure as president, while Henry Kissinger remembers Washington as "a besieged city" with the White House surrounded by district buses and elements of the 82nd Airborne hidden in the Executive Office Building awaiting who knows what—the "very fabric of government was falling apart," during that period, while another aide remembers the press secretary declaring, "We're at war."[9]

The situation had gotten out of hand. On May 6, Nixon sent condolence letters to the parents of the students killed at Kent State; two days later he met with eight university presidents, and on May 11, with the nation's governors. In addition, he appointed Alexander Heard, the president of Vanderbilt University, his special adviser on university affairs and sent teams of aides to campuses to listen to students and faculty. At the same time, members of his inner circle held numerous meetings with young people and dissenters, which included a celebrated confrontation between Kissinger and his former Harvard University colleagues, which ended up in a shouting match. Earlier in April, the national security advisor had stormed out of an appearance at Johns Hopkins University when the first questioner asked, "Dr. Kissinger, do you consider yourself a war criminal?"[10]

The Democratic Congress was up in arms as well. The Senate revoked the Gulf of Tonkin Resolution during this period and, more important, passed the Cooper-Church amendment (by a vote of 58–37 with 16 Republicans joining the majority), which threatened to cut off funds for the war if all American troops had not withdrawn from Cambodia by June 30. The House rejected the amendment and Nixon never confronted the challenge from the Senate because he claimed that he had no intention of keeping troops in Cambodia beyond June 30.

More troublesome was the McGovern-Hatfield amendment that called for cutting off of all funding by December 31, which made its way through the Senate. That amendment was defeated in September by a 55–39 vote, helped in good measure by the White House's secret organization of a lobby, Americans for Winning the Peace, which energetically opposed the legislation in over twenty-five cities.

THE ORGANIZED ANTIWAR MOVEMENT, LED BY THE NEW MOBE, HURriedly called for a protest against the Cambodian invasion for the weekend of May 9–10. Although doves did not have enough time to obtain rally permits, the government waived the fifteen-day period fearing that tens of thousands would show up to protest, permits or not. Considering the short planning time and the interminable squabbles between the sectarians over tactics, it was amazing that at least 100,000 demonstrators appeared in Washington that weekend. Trying to organize a protest against bombing of Afghanistan in 2001, one organizer marveled at the way his predecessors were able to bring so many people together so quickly—"I don't understand how Vietnam got organized the way it did. Without the Internet, there's no way we could have gotten 17 colleges on board in two weeks."[11]

Planning for the Cambodian protest was so chaotic, however, that up to the last moment leaders were not certain what they were going to do beyond arranging for scores of speeches and music. Most of the squabbles revolved around the desire on the part of some activists to perform organized acts of civil disobedience. David Dellinger, as usual an advocate of non-violent civil disobedience, recalled, "There was so much confusion. . . . It was all so uncertain. . . . We were split right up to the end."[12] An ambitious plan for civil disobedience, which never materialized after the formal rally, was to have involved thousands of protesters who were to deliver symbolic caskets to the White House and who then would stage a massive sit-in around the building and in neighboring streets. The outrage over Cambodia was so intense throughout the nation that such a model might have been spontaneously replicated in other cities. Strategists later suggested that May 1970 and not May 1971, when such activities did take place in Washington, would have been the best time to test such a tactic, given the unpopularity of the Cambodian invasion among a significant portion of the population and the media.

Benjamin Spock chaired the rally at the Ellipse behind the White House, where he was joined by nine congresspersons on the platform; scores of their colleagues participated more anonymously in the crowd.

John Froines, one of the defendants in the Chicago Eight trial, led a "Fuck Nixon" chant that did not amuse most of the adults in the crowd. Journalists reported that a good number of the White college students, who made up the largest portion of the protesters, were attending their first antiwar rally. Several hundred federal employees took up positions on the Ellipse behind a banner that read, "Federal Bums Against the War." In another action in the capital, Peace Corps volunteers briefly took over six offices in their building, which they labeled "Ho Chi Minh Sanctuary," and flew a Vietcong flag from one of the windows. The flag could be seen from the White House.

Other rallies were held around the country with attendance figures of 50,000 in Minneapolis, 60,000 in Chicago, 20,000 in Austin, and 12,000 in San Diego. Most of the participants were not radicals but concerned college students who were angered by the apparent expansion of a war that the president said was winding down and by the killings at Kent State.

The most unusual event of the Washington weekend took place on the eve of the demonstration. Richard Nixon had been in an anxious mood. Between 10:35 P.M. and 3:50 A.M. on the evening of May 8 and the early morning of May 9, he made more than fifty phone calls, including eight to Kissinger and seven to Haldeman. Around 5 A.M., he suddenly left the White House, accompanied only by his valet, to journey to the area around the Lincoln Memorial where thousands of students were camping out awaiting that day's events. This spontaneous early morning jaunt caught his chief aides unawares and greatly concerned the Secret Service, which hastily dispatched a contingent of agents to protect him from potential attack.

Nixon wandered around the Memorial talking to bleary-eyed students about the war, college, foreign travel, their home towns, and also about football. He claimed he went to see them because he wanted to hear what they had to say and also to demonstrate that he sympathized with their concerns. When students were interviewed later they and the media stressed the president's flippant remarks about college athletics and travel rather than the more serious conversations about the war, which he claimed constituted the vast majority of his comments. This apparently skewed report concerned the White House; one aide noted, "Rambling talk in Memorial might hurt."[13]

The media were not especially impressed with the speakers at the demonstrations in Washington and elsewhere that weekend, although they were impressed with the earnest young people who attended them. According to the left-wing *Village Voice*, for example, the speakers at the Ellipse who offered stale speeches were boring—it was "just another Mobe picnic," while to *Time* it was a "canned rally." Other journalists noted the difficulty many in the crowd had hearing the speeches, and, in any event, their lack of interest in the harangues, or as the *Washington Post* headlined its story, "It Was Just Too Hot for a Revolution."[14] The television networks did offer live remotes from the demonstration during the day, with NBC presenting special broadcasts both before and after its baseball game of the week. No previous demonstration had received such relatively generous treatment in terms of live coverage. In this case, with the air of crisis hanging over Washington, it seemed appropriate. More important, antiwar activity received a boost when the television-network news shows concentrated on interviews with clean-cut college students at their first rally.

Nixon's media monitors were not pleased by what they saw on those shows. They noted that editorially the seven media that counted the most, the three television networks, the *New York Times*, *Washington Post*, *Time*, and *Newsweek*, strongly opposed the invasion of Cambodia. They were also disheartened by their private poll, which showed that while 45 percent considered student dissent to be a serious problem, 41 percent approved of it. Among that 41 percent were 57 percent of all the young people in the poll and 53 percent of those who were college-educated. One bright spot for the administration was the fact that most Americans drew the line at student strikes.

In June, Nixon asked former Pennsylvania governor William Scranton, a liberal Republican with a dovish son, to chair a Commission on Campus Unrest, loading the dice with his instructions, "Don't let higher education off with a pat on the ass,"[15] but he was disappointed with Scranton's report completed later that year. Although the commission was critical of violence on campus, it sympathized with the concerns of students, most of whom it found to be serious, non-revolutionary, and peaceful in their protest activities.

NIXON RODE OUT THE STORM OF HIS CAMBODIAN INVASION. BY JUNE 30, when he announced the pull-out of all American troops and an exaggerated claim to a great victory over the North Vietnamese by capturing weapons and materiel and destroying infrastructures (but not COSVN), he and his administration had regained their confidence. For one thing, colleges had shut down for the summer and more importantly, many students had recoiled from the events of the period that saw, from their perspective, a government willing to kill protesters, and colleges closed—leaving them high and dry in terms of obtaining degrees and finishing classes.

In addition, while the majority of college students sympathized with the antiwar activities of their colleagues, much of the rest of the country did not. Characteristic of this feeling was the attack on May 8 by a group of New York "hardhats," on antiwar protesters, some of whom carried Vietcong flags. This activity led to a formal pro-administration demonstration in New York on May 20, encouraged by the White House, which drew as many as 100,000 predominantly labor-union members. Six days later, Nixon greeted a group of the marchers in the White House. Their leader, Peter Brennan, became secretary of labor in 1973.

The president's appeal to patriotism and American values appeared to be working as he energized his Silent Majority once again. Celebrated evangelist Billy Graham, who appeared with his friend at a large rally in a stadium in Knoxville, Tennessee on April 28, helped his cause. And the tiny minority of foul-mouthed protesters in the crowd who were captured by television cameras also helped. On July 4, Nixon sponsored an Honor America Day in Washington, with Bob Hope, Red Skelton, and the Mormon Tabernacle Choir appearing before 500,000 onlookers. Many of those in the crowd would have joined the 58 percent of their fellow citizens who told pollsters they blamed the students for what had happened at Kent State. More joined them in those sentiments after hearing about the killing of an innocent student when four radicals bombed the Army Math Research Center Building on the campus of the University of Wisconsin on August 28. Although the killing was not in their plans since the bombers expected the building to be empty in the middle of the night, they declared they needed "to bring the war home, we had to make a dent in the war machine."[16] The Research Center action followed on the heels of sensational Weathermen bombings of the police department and the Bank of America in New York in June and August.

Later that year, FBI Director J. Edgar Hoover announced that he had uncovered a conspiracy involving Philip Berrigan and seven others who were allegedly planning to blow up power ducts under the

Capitol and to kidnap a top official, later revealed to be Henry Kissinger. An informant who shared a cell with Berrigan gave the information to the FBI. The charges were eventually dropped after the first trial ended in a hung jury in April 1972. (One of the conspirators' lawyers was former Attorney General Ramsey Clark.) By the end of 1970, however, many Americans believed that radicals would attempt such a plot.

The tables were ultimately turned on the FBI the following March when unknown burglars broke into one of its offices in Media, Pennsylvania, and took thousand of files revealing shocking illegal actions committed by agents in pursuit of radicals and other dissenters. Those files soon found their way into the national media. Of course, many people in the United States had become so distressed about radicalism and violence that they saw little wrong with the violation of civil liberties to protect national security.

The disruptions on campus following the Cambodian invasion and Kent State killings also contributed to Nixon's aborted attempt to establish a new secret super-intelligence agency directed from the White House. He was unhappy with the work being done by the CIA and the FBI to monitor radicals and leftists on campuses and elsewhere. Under the Huston Plan approved by the president in June, but never put into operation because of FBI opposition, Nixon hoped to improve domestic intelligence gathering and proactive harassing of his political enemies. Even without the plan, the intelligence community's stepped-up activities against radicals from 1970 through 1973 led to Justice Department subpoenas for 2,000 witnesses to appear before 100 grand juries in 84 cities in 36 states. Further, with a change in the leadership of the IRS, Nixon's chief of staff Bob Haldeman gloated, "Now that we have our man in the IRS, he wants to pull the Clark Clifford file and also the top supporters of the doves."[17] Appearances before grand juries and IRS auditors may not all have produced convictions or fines, but they did result in occupying the energies and resources of movement leaders.

CONSIDERING WHAT WAS THEN GOING ON IN THE RADICAL COMMUNITY, Nixon did not need the Huston Plan or even intensified intelligence and harassment operations to weaken his enemies. The antiwar movement was once again in disarray as the New Mobe came apart

in the weeks following the Cambodian demonstration, in good measure because of the conflict among its organizers. As one activist
lamented, "The movement tore itself apart even though it had won a
victory. We got a hundred thousand people there in a week's time. . . .
Nixon got on television and said he was going to pull all the troops
out [of Cambodia] in thirty [sic] days. I thought we'd won."[18]

The major issue, as usual, was the form of the next round of
protests. Opponents of the war had tried everything they could by this
point including self-immolation, bombings, tax and draft resistance,
mass demonstrations, electoral politics, and petitioning and lobbying,
but still the war continued. One leader wrote to another in the early
fall, "There is a lot of self-searching going on. . . . The Weatherman
timetable is too short, leading to desperate acts. We need a timetable
longer than theirs but shorter than the liberal reformers."[19] Others
were debilitated. The Reverend William Sloan Coffin later explained,
"I was tired of the whole affair. I was fed up with the war . . . and I
was tired of fighting Nixon."[20]

One of the key political groups in the Mobe leadership, the Socialist Workers Party, had refused to accept their colleagues' suggestions
for expanding tactics beyond peaceful rallies and marches and for
broadening the appeal of the antiwar movement by embracing other
left-wing causes, which would not be supported by many liberals. In
addition, the SWP took issue with the lack of discipline and organization of their coalition colleagues. Thus, it formed its own new peace
coalition, the National Peace Action Coalition (NPAC) in June, which
would continue the struggle exclusively through single-issue, decorous
antiwar demonstrations. In December, it decided to hold another mass
demonstration in Washington on April 24.

In November more radical elements of the New Mobe launched
the National Committee Against War, Racism, and Repression, which
embraced different strategies and tactics. That group, whose leadership included Sidney Peck, Dellinger, Brad Lyttle, Rennie Davis, and
the Fifth Avenue Peace Parade Committee, changed its name to the
People's Committee for Peace and Justice (PCPJ) in February. It planned
actions for Washington in early May with one of its allies, the May
Day Collective (later Tribe), leading an experiment in the sort of massive disobedience that had been contemplated in the Cambodia/Kent
State demonstration. The Collective planned to "raise the cost of the
war . . . to create the spectre of social chaos" by closing down the gov-

ernment.[21] Interestingly, although both new coalitions maintained offices in the same building in Washington, feelings were so intense that "no one talked to anyone in the elevator."[22]

For their part, moderate organizations in the antiwar camp, SANE, the ADA, and the New Democratic Coalition, concentrated their immediate attention on the 1970 congressional elections in a program called "Referendum 70," which worked with the National Coalition for a Responsible Congress. Others joined the Princeton based Movement for a New Congress, which provided student campaign workers for antiwar candidates. In May, a Bipartisan Congressional Clearing House, supported by forty organizations, had been established to identify dovish candidates in the election. By this juncture, a majority of members of the Democratic Party called themselves doves.

Antiwar candidates needed all the help they could get given that Nixon had begun a vigorous campaign to elect Republicans who supported administration policy. He instructed his aides to "Emphasize-anti-Crime-anti-Demonstrations, anti-Drug, anti-Obscenity-Get in touch with the mood of the country which is fed up with the Liberals."[23] The enemy, he told chief campaigner, Vice President Spiro T. Agnew, were the "Radiclibs." According to Haldeman, campus unrest was "the key issue of the campaign."[24]

When the polls revealed that his approach was not working, Nixon himself went on the road to promote his candidates, visiting twenty-three states during the final two weeks of the campaign. His aides liked to permit small groups of antiwar protesters into the president's rallies to "give the president the opportunity to strike out at them."[25] On October 29, after an appearance in San Jose, California, he was surrounded by a mob that had been chanting "One, two, three, four, we don't want your fuckin' war." Some demonstrators threw rocks at the president in what William Safire called, "a mob attack on a U.S. President, unique in our history."[26] Nixon had encouraged the attack by jumping on the hood of his limousine and flashing the hostile crowd his trademark "V" sign. He said he simply "could not resist showing them how little respect [he] had for their juvenile and mindless ranting."[27]

He used the attack on his person in the final speeches of the campaign, appealing again to the Silent Majority to replace representatives who were soft on such brutish behavior. His well-financed, full-press attack on liberal Democrats produced mixed results. In the Senate, three prominent doves were defeated as the Democrats lost two seats overall. But in the House, the Democrats gained nine seats, and of the twelve representatives who were not returned, ten had been support-ive of the administration's Vietnam policy.

During the same period, CALC intensified its campaigns in the business community. CALC members who owned stock attended annual stockholders' meetings to demand "corporate responsibility," which meant that the companies should desist from participating in the war. Such was the case with Operation Honeywell, which the organization had launched in 1968 to convince that corporation to stop supplying the Pentagon with anti-personnel bombs. Another approach was that adopted by the Ann Arbor City Council several years later when it banned city managers from buying any products made by Honeywell. In October, 1970 CALC began publishing its own weekly eight-page newspaper, *American Report,* which reached a cir-culation of 24,000 by 1972.

In addition, FOR, SANE, and CALC sponsored a new organiza-tion, the Interfaith Committee to Set the Date (later Set the Date Now), which called for an end to the war by July 4, 1971. Twenty House members who traveled around the country promoting the idea joined them. When it did not immediately catch fire, the date for ending the war was pushed back to December 31, 1971. Among Johnson admin-istration loyalists who campaigned for setting the date were Clark Clif-ford, Paul Warnke, and Averell Harriman.

In September, 150 members of the rapidly growing Vietnam Vet-erans Against the War (VVAW) participated in Operation Raw (Raw stood for Rapid American Withdrawal and was War spelled back-wards), a march from Morristown, New Jersey to Valley Forge, Penn-sylvania during which they simulated search-and-destroy missions in Vietnam and performed guerrilla theater. The flyer they handed out after their actions read in part,

> A U.S. Infantry company just came through here. If you had been Viet-namese—we might have burned your house, we might have shot your dog, we might have shot you, we might have raped your wife and your daughter. . . . Help us to end the war before they turn your son into a butcher or a corpse.[28]

Finally, as had been the case since 1965, individuals in thousands of venues continued to express antiwar positions in a variety of ways, such as the Miss Montana, Kathy Huppe, who gave up her title when directors of the Miss America pageant demanded that she stop speaking out against the war.

BY THE END OF 1970, THERE WERE STILL 335,000 U.S. TROOPS IN Vietnam, but the number of battle deaths suffered by Americans had declined from almost 2,900 during the first half of the year to about 1,350 during the second half. The war was winding down for most Americans, a fact that made it more difficult for those who demanded immediate withdrawal or even merely a shorter timetable to attract support. The president had promised he would end the war in an honorable way and claimed to be on his way toward that goal. Whether or not he wanted to slow the pace of American withdrawal from Vietnam, once those withdrawals started there was no holding back, especially considering the increasingly low morale, lack of discipline, and rise in the use of drugs among American recruits in Vietnam. Secretary of Defense Melvin Laird expressed "shock" by what he saw on a visit to Vietnam in January 1971—the situation was far worse than he had been led to believe.[29]

Many of the morale and discipline problems stemmed from the type of "dirty" counter-guerrilla war that Americans felt compelled to wage. In December 1970, a group calling itself the Citizens' Commission of Inquiry into U.S. War Crimes in Vietnam held hearings in Washington in which veterans and others testified about atrocities committed in Vietnam. The issue of atrocities committed by the military had long been central to the antiwar opposition of many Americans. Periodically, the mainstream media offered stories about seemingly unnecessary civilian deaths in both North and South Vietnam attributed to American artillery and bombs. In the summer of 1967, for example, Jonathan Schell's *New Yorker* report about "The Village of Ben Suc," affected many Americans, including, it was rumored, Secretary of Defense McNamara.

From January 31 through February 2, 1971, the VVAW held its own hearings in Detroit, where more than 100 veterans offered eyewitness testimony to the bloody atrocities they had seen or had committed. The VVAW or Winter Soldier hearings were financed, among others, by CALC, BEM, Emil Mazey of the UAW, the rock group Crosby, Stills, and Nash, and, especially, actress Jane Fonda who lived in Detroit for several months while she helped to organize them.

("Winter Soldier" was a play on Thomas Paine's summer soldier or "sunshine patriot" who left the American side during the American Revolution when the going got rough.) Although Senator Mark Hatfield, a Republican from Oregon, read the Winter Soldier transcript into the *Congressional Record,* the Detroit hearings attracted little media attention. Part of the reason was the counterattack offered by veterans' groups, backed by the administration, falsely claiming that most of those who testified were imposters who had never seen combat in Vietnam. The VVAW was so distressed by the response that it began planning an even more dramatic activity for Washington in the spring. The veterans were assisted by *Playboy* magazine, which gave them a free, full-page advertisement to promote their cause. The ad produced inquiries from more than 1,000 active-duty personnel who wanted to join the organization.

Those who brought up the issue of atrocities had more evidence when Lt. William Calley was brought to trial in March 1971 for the My Lai Massacre. After the trial, few Americans doubted that a massacre, at which U.S. soldiers executed over 300 innocent civilians, happened. Many sympathized with Calley, however, either because he was following orders or because such actions were understandable when you were up against evil Communist guerrillas who did not fight cleanly themselves, as seen most prominently in their massacre of several thousand civilians in Hue during the Tet Offensive. Those who contended that the United States should be held to a higher moral standard than the Communists weakened that argument. Some on the left also sympathized with Calley since none of Pentagon brass who had covered up the massacre were punished.

One other military matter, the fate of the POWs in North Vietnam, complicated problems for those trying to pressure the administration into ending the war sooner than it desired. Playing upon the widespread support for the POWs who were being held in extremely difficult conditions and about whom the North Vietnamese offered little information, the president used as one of his excuses for lack of movement in negotiations, Hanoi's unwillingness both to account for them and to promise that they would all be returned at war's end. Thus, anyone who called for immediate withdrawal appeared to be unsympathetic to the fate of the POWs, whose families and support groups enjoyed a favorable image in the media.

IN AN EERIE REPLAY OF THE PERIOD FROM THE MORATORIUM TO THE Cambodia invasion, the administration felt that it had recovered enough from the Cambodian debacle that it could once again attempt to prod the enemy through escalating tactics. In this case, it was an incursion on February 8 into Laos, which like Cambodia, was host to part of the Ho Chi Minh Trail. In a tribute to the latent power of the antiwar movement and also to the general concern among the public about American casualties, the Laos operation involved South Vietnamese troops with Americans playing only a support role. The U.S. military in Vietnam did not think that Vietnamization had proceeded far enough to justify an all South Vietnamese attack against Communist positions in Laos. But there was no option this time—the administration was not prepared to experience another firestorm such as that which had greeted it the previous May. As most on-the-scene observers had predicted, the invasion was a failure. The South Vietnamese were precipitously withdrawn in full view of television cameras showing them so anxious to escape the combat theater that they were clinging to helicopter struts. Kissinger was furious. "Those sons of bitches," he railed, "It's their country and we can't save it for them if they don't want to."[30]

In part because no Americans were involved and because the invasion took place in the winter, reaction from the antiwarriors to another apparent escalation lacked vigor. As few as 50,000 gathered nationwide to protest in events that were generally lackluster and barely covered by the media. The problem was that by 1971 demonstrations had become so common that unless the numbers attending broke records or the participants used dramatic new tactics, it was not "news." What was news was the March 1 bombing of a bathroom in the Senate by the Weathermen—an action that certainly did not help the antiwar movement when an anonymous spokesperson claimed that they were doing it because of Laos. All the same, in the wake of the invasion, by 46 to 41 percent, Americans disapproved of the way the president was handling the war, and, in March, 69 percent of those polled believed that the administration was not telling them all that they needed to know about the war.

The administration was rocked again on March 28, 1971, when former *New York Times* Vietnam correspondent, Neil Sheehan, reviewed thirty-three books for that paper's influential Sunday book-review section under the headline, "Should We Have War Crimes Trials?" After a careful review of the evidence, he concluded yes. The Calley verdict was made public the next day. Three days later, 400 college-student presidents and editors issued an open letter to the president strongly opposing his policies in Vietnam. The stage was set for the last major series of antiwar demonstrations that took place in Washington from April 19 through the first week of May.

NOTES

1. William Safire, *Before the Fall: An Inside View of the Pre-Watergate White House* (Garden City, NJ: Doubleday, 1975), 308.

2. Zaroulis and Sullivan, *Who Spoke Up?* 309.

3. Seymour Hersh, *The Price of Power: Kissinger in the White House* (New York: Simon and Schuster, 1983), 191.

4. Charles Colson, *Born Again* (Old Tappan, NJ: Chosen Books, 1976), 34.

5. Wells, *The War Within,* 424.

6. Ibid., 421.

7. Robbie Lieberman and David Cochran, "We Closed Down the School: The Party Culture at Southern Illinois University during the Vietnam War Era," in *Peace and Change* 16 (July 2001): 326.

8. Small, *The Presidency of Richard Nixon,* 79.

9. Nixon, RN, 457; Henry Kissinger, *White House Years* (Boston: Little, Brown, 1979), 511; Zaroulis and Sullivan, *Who Spoke Up?* 329; Small, *Johnson, Nixon, and the Doves,* 203.

10. Hersh, *The Price of Power,* 196n.

11. *New York Times,* November 21, 2001, B8.

12. Wells, *The War Within,* 442.

13. Small, *Covering Dissent,* 138.

14. Ibid., 135, 136.

15. Wells, *The War Within,* 448.

16. Anderson, *The Movement,* 367.

17. H. R. Haldeman, *The Haldeman Diaries: Inside the Nixon White House* (New York: G. P. Putnam's Sons, 1994), 305.

18. Wells, *The War Within,* 447.

19. DeBenedetti, *An American Ordeal,* 297.

20. William Sloane Coffin, *Once to Every Man: A Memoir* (New York: Atheneum, 1977), 308.

21. Wells, *The War Within,* 471.

22. DeBenedetti, *An American Ordeal,* 302.

23. Stephen E. Ambrose, *Nixon: The Triumph of a Politician: 1962–1972* (New York: Simon and Schuster, 1989), 374.

24. Wells, *The War Within,* 459.

25. Mann, *Grand Delusion*, 674.

26. Safire, *Before the Fall*, 332.

27. Nixon, RN, 492.

28. Gerald Nicosia, *Home to War: A History of the Vietnam Veterans' Movement* (New York: Crown, 2001), 61.

29. Wells, *The War Within*, 475.

30. William Hammond, *Public Affairs: The Military and the Media, 1968-1975* (Washington: Center of Military History, 1996), 468.

CHAPTER Eight

THE WAR AND THE MOVEMENT WIND DOWN

T HE THREE DIFFERENT ANTIWAR ACTIVITIES THAT TOOK PLACE in Washington from April 19 through May 5, 1971, constitute one of the most instructive protest periods in American history for those interested in antiwar movements and indeed, in dissent in any modern society. The first and unique activity that took place from April 19 through April 23, was Operation Dewey Canyon III, the "invasion" of Washington by 2,000 VVAW members who lobbied and performed symbolic acts of protest. On Saturday, April 24, there followed what may have been the largest single rally in the history of the antiwar movement. On May 3 the advocates of mass, non-violent civil disobedience finally had their chance as 30,000 of their number began a three-day attempt to shut down Washington through the obstruction of the city's thorough-fares. The responses to these different forms of dissent from the media, the public, and the administration help one understand the strengths and weaknesses of the antiwar movement as both it and the war wound down.

EXASPERATED BY THEIR FAILURE TO ATTRACT ATTENTION WITH THE Winter Soldier hearings, the VVAW planned several different events during their five days in Washington from April 19 through 23. Dressed in fatigues with their battle ribbons attached, some in wheel chairs or on crutches, they began arriving in the capital on April 17 at an informal encampment on the Mall. VVAW leaders had not received permission for the camp-in. Thus, the Justice Department obtained an order from a judge to evict the "trespassers." But at the last moment, the administration decided not to use force to remove wounded and other veterans from the Mall in full view of television cameras and, in any event, a federal court soon revoked the department's injunction.

The first few days of Operation Dewey Canyon III (the first two Dewey Canyons were offensives in South Vietnam) or "a limited incursion into the country of Congress," included scores of telegenic activities from street theater, in which khaki-clad veterans simulated search-and-destroy missions, to the veterans' failed attempts to turn themselves in as war criminals, to visit their comrades' graves in Arlington National Cemetery, and to plead their case before the Supreme Court. After being barred from the cemetery because of a prohibition against political demonstrations, they ran into a delegate from the Daughters of the American Revolution Convention that happened to be in town. She told one vet, "Son, I don't think what you are doing is good for the troops." He replied, "Lady, we are the troops."[1] At the court, when 110 veterans were arrested for refusing to leave the premises, they surrendered POW style with their hands held over their heads. Instead of carrying Vietcong flags like other doves, they carried American flags. They were quickly acquitted of all charges.

On Capitol Hill, John Kerry, a clean-cut and articulate Navy veteran who had been wounded three times, offered compelling testimony to the Senate Foreign Relations Committee. Later elected a Democratic senator from Massachusetts, Kerry cut an imposing figure as he explained,

> The country doesn't realize it yet but it has created a monster in the form of thousands of men who have been taught to deal and to trade in violence and who are given the chance to die for the biggest nothing in history—men have returned with a sense of anger and betrayal that no one so far has been able to grasp.[2]

A fitting climax to the week full of evocative VVAW demonstrations was the emotional protest on April 23 in front of the Capitol where over 600 veterans threw their combat medals and ribbons—

"symbols of shame," they claimed—over the fence and onto the Capitol lawn. A small group of them had performed a similar act outside the White House on Lincoln's Birthday. On this occasion, most of the vets made brief comments about the reasons for returning their awards and often dedicated the action to fallen comrades. These highly personal statements, some of which were captured in moving sound bites on the network news shows, provided one of the most dramatic moments in the history of the antiwar movement. Voices cracked with anger and sorrow and tears flowed freely, not only among the participants but those who watched in person or on their television screens. Most poignant were the vets who appeared in wheelchairs, on crutches, or with missing limbs.

Just as it appeared that the antiwarriors had exhausted all protest forms, along came the VVAW to demonstrate once again the inventiveness of the movement. It also demonstrated that the size of an antiwar action was not always the most important variable in determining its impact on opinion. The administration counterattacked against what it correctly perceived to be an effective protest. The campaign to defame the VVAW, titled in an internal memo "Non-Veterans Demonstration," used the head of the Veterans of Foreign Wars to assert that many of those participating were not veterans. The VVAW leadership admitted that some of the people supporting their activities in Washington were not veterans but asserted that it had registered 2,300 veterans of whom 93 percent had been in the combat theater. The actual number of vets participating each day was probably closer to 1,200. One veteran, in *Time* magazine's favorable account of "simple eloquence," introduced his glass eye into evidence as proof of his combat wound.[3]

The administration's counterattack had failed and it knew it, even though it had placed informants in the VVAW's leadership cadre. It began when the Justice Department failed to eject the veterans from the Mall because of the fear of unfavorable treatment from the media who seemed hopelessly enamored of the veterans. They were not necessarily enamored of the veterans themselves; they were enamored of a new form of protest that made for a compelling story line and exciting visuals. Haldeman complained that the "media by their own obsession created a major thing out of what should have been almost totally ignored." Another aide noted, the "media are killing us—what can we do? . . . [the networks] run the Vets every nite," while another joined in, "How can we fight back? . . . against the "impact of 5 days of Vets as lead story."[4]

It is difficult to determine that impact. Most people who saw the VVAW on television or in their print media were likely to have been impressed. Despite their long hair and generally disheveled appearance, they were not, after all, hippies or spoiled college students. It is also likely that hundreds of thousands of other veterans who privately shared the views of the VVAW became emboldened by the Washington actions to express their own antiwar sentiments, especially those who had served in Vietnam after 1967 when morale began to disintegrate. At the least, VVAW's membership increased from 10,000 to 20,000 from 1971 to 1972. Yet one wonders how such activities in the spring of 1971 affected American attitudes toward Nixon's policies in Vietnam. By that juncture, most Americans had made up their minds about the pace of troop withdrawals. As long as Nixon did not try another Cambodia, it is difficult to imagine that many more citizens would be attracted to the movement because of new pleadings and demonstrations from activists, even if, like the VVAW, they viewed them sympathetically.

That may have been the reason why those who attended the largest single demonstration in American history in Washington on Saturday, April 24, seemed to lack spirit, almost resigned to the likelihood that the president was not going to change his policy because of them and more important, they were not going to win over the majority of the population to their call for an end to the war sooner rather than later. At least 300,000 and perhaps as many as 500,000 showed up that day to march from the Ellipse down Pennsylvania Avenue to the Capitol where organizers had obtained permission to use the Capitol steps for a rally, the first time that such permission had been granted. (In San Francisco the same day, at least 150,000 came out to protest, including comedian-activist Dick Gregory who vowed to fast until the war was over, but the largest rally in West Coast history was cut short when militants seized the platform.)

According to one survey, as many as one-third of those in Washington were attending their first antiwar rally. Most of those interviewed expressed frustration and even pessimism about convincing the administration to withdraw from Vietnam. *Time* referred to a "layer of despair" that hung over the assemblage.[5] More middle-class adults turned up at this march than at previous ones and one could spot more union banners and black faces in the crowd than had been the norm.

One fifty-four-year-old man proclaimed, "I am a member of the Silent Majority who isn't that silent anymore."[6] Not all the coverage was positive. As had become more common, although this NPAC event was organized around a single theme, protesters who carried banners promoting anti-Zionism, Black Power, Gay Liberation, and other controversial causes offended many who viewed photos of the demonstration.

The immense size of the crowd and the wide variety of people who showed up represented almost as bad a tactical defeat for the administration as was its failure to counter the friendly media coverage the VVAW received. After all, Attorney General John Mitchell offered several press conferences during the week preceding the march predicting violence, a prediction that should have kept many of the middle-class first-timers at home.

Among the speakers who made their way to the lectern during the five-hour rally were responsible members of the liberal establishment such as Senators Gruening and Hartke, two New York representatives, Bella Abzug and Herman Badillo, John Kerry, and Coretta Scott King. Aside from Abzug and Badillo, twenty-four other members of Congress endorsed the demonstration. Four of their number chose April 24 to introduce a House resolution supporting the People's Peace Treaty. Mainstream pop artist John Denver was among those who provided the entertainment. Although revolutionary types were present on the fringes of the event, the police made only ten arrests.

Those who expected to see all or some of the largest demonstration in American history live on their television sets were disappointed. The tiny National Educational Network did cover the entire event, but the commercial networks offered no live remotes as they had during the Cambodian/Kent State demonstration the previous year. As usual, network executives explained that they refrained from presenting live coverage because of the need to provide equal time for the other side and because they feared that live cameras would provoke "crazies" to perform unlawful acts. No doubt the fact that there was no crisis atmosphere, as there had been during the previous May, and the notion that if you've seen one demonstration, you've seen them all informed the networks' decisions. The Washington rally was no longer "news," even if it drew the largest crowd in American history. Journalists had seen the "largest crowd in . . ." at several earlier demonstrations.

On their regular newscasts, however, the networks treated the rally quite positively with generous amounts of airtime during which reporters emphasized the size and the gentle nature of the huge assemblage. Yet, they had observed such demonstrations before, as they, according to the *Washington Post,* had become a "staple" in the capital with a predictable rhythm to the events of the day.[7] So predictable were they that one reporter explained that he did not devote much space to the speeches because the messages had been heard before.

The administration was not as upset by the media's relatively favorable treatment of the demonstration, as compared to the VVAW activities, since while it was impressive, it was according to one aide, "big but w/o balls."[8] Nixon, who had monitored the event virtually hour by hour from Camp David, had little to fear since he agreed with the media view that this antiwar rally was just another among many that had little effect on most of the people who saw or read about it. However, he did worry that news of the largest antiwar rally in American history would encourage Hanoi.

AFTER THE RALLY, SOME OF THE PARTICIPANTS STAYED ON IN WASHington, camping out in public parks, churches, and dormitories. They and others who joined them participated in a "People's Lobby" over the next week, staging pray-ins, acting in guerrilla theater, appearing at legislators' offices dressed as Vietnamese peasants, and making visits to the IRS, the CIA, and Social Security System, where they tried to convince government employees to stop supporting the war effort. During this period, someone even hung an NLF flag on Secretary of Defense Laird's front porch in Bethesda, Maryland.

These were small actions compared with those planned by the May Day Tribe whose "members" tried to shut down Washington during the week that started on Monday May 3. The tribe contended that it could stop the war machine by making it impossible for the bureaucrats in charge of the war to get to work or move between offices. They had already made their peace, the "People's Peace Treaty," with Vietnamese students—the war was over and the Nixon administration had failed to recognize it.

Sponsored by the PCPJ and led by Rennie Davis, the non-violent "civil disobedients" planned to sit down in streets, block bridges with their bodies, and otherwise impede traffic in large enough numbers to overwhelm the district police and judicial system. Considering the number of government workers who came into the District over a very few bridges from Virginia and a handful of major thoroughfares from Maryland, it appeared that thousands of protesters could at the very least seriously disrupt the government's operations, if not shut it down entirely. But it was hard to keep a secret in a cadre of 30,000 that had been penetrated by intelligence agencies.

The administration geared up for battle in a variety of ways. Aside from the police, soldiers in flak jackets, backed up by helicopters, had been called in to suppress the demonstration. The night before the May Day Tribe's action, the police routed its followers from their campgrounds following an all-night rock concert. At the same time, White House counsel John Dean had prepared a document for the president, just in case he needed it, to take extraordinary measures akin to martial law to protect government workers and their buildings. Assistant Attorney General William Rehnquist certified the constitutionality of the proposed measures.

Nixon did not need to use Dean's document, even though the forces of authority behaved as if the president had declared martial law. In the first place, that Monday, government workers were ordered to come in to work in the early morning hours before the civil disobedience began. More important, after first trying to disperse the protesters with tear gas and clubs, the police and military began to ignore the Constitution, and executed grand sweeps in which everyone in an affected area was arrested, not read their rights, and then consigned to makeshift detention centers, such as the football field outside RFK Stadium, where they languished without benefit of arraignment. That illegal tactic was the key to the administration's success. During the first two hours on Monday morning 2,000 people were arrested; by noon 7,000 had been taken into custody, a minority of whom had been ordinary citizens who happened to be in the wrong place at the wrong time, in the largest mass arrest in American history. Although scores of streets were temporarily blockaded with cars, trashcans, and other obstacles, with several young people even trying to remove distributor caps from cars waiting at intersections, Washington was not closed down.

Conditions in the detention centers were abysmal, with not enough toilet facilities and little food. Nixon aide Charles Colson did secretly send the prisoners a crate of oranges, "compliments" of Senator

Edmund Muskie of Maine, the president's chief Democratic rival at
the time. Scores of black citizens of Washington, who lived near the
main detention center, brought food to the young people in a genuine
gesture of solidarity.

Despite months of planning, the May Day Tribe's execution was
sloppy, owing to some degree to leader Rennie Davis's "burn out" that
some of his friends considered a full-blown nervous breakdown. For
example, while the May Day people were trying to close the Fourteenth
Street Bridge to Virginia, their allies in the PCPJ, led by Benjamin
Spock, were trying to cross that bridge on a planned march from the
Washington Monument to the Pentagon. One of those maced and
arrested in the melee that followed was a former Kissinger aide named
Daniel Ellsberg. A PCPJ leader had to admit on May 3 that "It was an
exciting concept, [but] it didn't work."[9] *Time* magazine concurred in
a story headlined, "Self Defeat for the 'Army of Peace,'" in which it
derided a "preposterously ill-organized" bunch of radicals.[10] Washington almost returned to normal on May 4, when only 685 people
were arrested. On May 5, five hundred federal employees rallied in
Lafayette Park in front of the White House, while at a demonstration
on the Capitol steps, 1,450 people were arrested.

In what one Nixon speechwriter referred to as a "military operation," more than 10,000 people had been arrested over a four-day
period.[11] According to him, the protesters were "Real beasts. . . . It
was a hate-filled kind of exercise."[12] In 1975, a federal court ruled that
the Nixon administration had violated the rights of those arrested and
the government had to pay monetary damages to 1,200 plaintiffs. But
that was four years later. In the meantime, the administration served
notice to those who wanted to try civil disobedience again that it could
successfully, if illegally, meet the challenge.

While few in the mainstream media depicted favorably the actions
of the May Day Tribe, by May 6, the story of the illegal arrests did
begin to appear in almost all publications to counterbalance the image
of the rag-tag, lawbreaking, civil disobedients. The majority of readers, however, accepted the administration's argument that when
national security is threatened, all constitutional niceties cannot be
observed. Nixon explained on June 1 that the police "showed a good
deal more concern for their [protesters'] rights than they showed for
the rights of the people of Washington."[13] While almost a third of those
polled had approved of the VVAW activity, only 18 percent approved

of the May Day assaults, and 56 percent endorsed the police methods employed in the capital.

Summing up the media coverage, the polls, and the failure of the dissidents to do any major damage, Colson concluded "This has really turned out to be a major plus for us."[14] Among other things, the firm hand displayed by the administration served as a lesson for those who might try such a tactic again. The May Day Tribe's offensive also played into Nixon's hands by underscoring the theme of his upcoming reelection campaign: the Democrats were the party of anarchy, hippies, and violence in the streets. On the other hand, that the movement was on the front pages of newspapers and appeared in lead stories on television newcasts for almost a three-week period meant that the war was not going away as an issue in American politics. A significant number of Americans, in some polls more than a majority, were not entirely pleased with Nixon's pace of withdrawal from Vietnam, while others who supported the president were concerned that the country was being torn apart by the disruptive tactics of the doves, some of whom were their children.

IT WAS NOT ONLY THE CHILDREN, HOWEVER. "THERE ARE FORCES AT work bent on destroying this government," lamented Henry Kissinger when hearing of the publication of excerpts from the "Pentagon Papers" in the *New York Times* on June 13, 1971.[15] The papers were a classified multi-volume history, commissioned by Secretary of Defense McNamara in 1967, examining American involvement in the Vietnam War. One of those working on the project, formally titled "History of U.S. Decision Making Process on Vietnam Policy," was Daniel Ellsberg, who had participated in the May Day disturbances the previous month. Ellsberg, a former Marine, civilian consultant in Vietnam, and consultant for Henry Kissinger, had become as ardent a dove as he once had been a hawk. He made an unauthorized copy of the history and, after failing to convince congresspersons to release it, settled on the *New York Times* and later the *Washington Post* as his outlets. The history, which did not cover the Nixon years, revealed that the Kennedy and Johnson administrations had not always leveled with the American people about the wars in Southeast Asia.

Kissinger in particular was outraged by the leak of classified material, which he claimed would make it impossible for the United States to conduct secret diplomacy in the future. He egged Nixon on to fight the publication of the documents because if he did not, "It shows you're a weakling, Mr. President."[16] On June 30, the Supreme Court ruled that the newspapers could publish the material. In order to punish Ellsberg and his cohort Anthony J. Russo as well as to discourage such leaks in the future, the administration brought an indictment against them for stealing government documents. More important, Nixon set out to destroy Ellsberg personally. When the FBI refused to assist in the project, the president set up his own intelligence operation, which became known as the Plumbers. They orchestrated a break-in at Ellsberg's psychiatrist's office in Beverly Hills in order to turn up damaging personal information on him. The operatives involved in the break-in were some of the same people involved in the break-in at Democratic headquarters in June 1972. One of the reasons for Nixon's notorious cover-up of the later break-in, which led to his resignation in August 1974 but about which he had little foreknowledge, was the need to cover-up the Ellsberg break-in about which he had a good deal of foreknowledge. Thus, the attempt to defame antiwar activist Ellsberg can be linked to the process that led to congressional investigations of the president and his resignation before he would be impeached and removed from office.

The closest the administration came to "punishing" Ellsberg was the recruitment of a group of Cuban-American thugs by Howard Hunt, a key figure in both break-ins, to assault him when he was giving a speech at an antiwar rally on the steps of the Capitol on May 3, 1972. The toughs never made it to Ellsberg, but they did manage to rough up others in the crowd. As for legal punishment, the case against Ellsberg and Russo was dismissed in 1973 after a judge learned about the administration's illegal harassment and surveillance.

In a related incident, in order to blackmail Lyndon Johnson into supporting him on the "Pentagon Papers" issue, Nixon ordered his aides to break into the Brookings Institution, where several former Johnson aides were working, to find Vietnam War related documents that might show that the 1968 bombing halt was politically motivated. Although Colson and Nixon aide G. Gordon Liddy drew up an imaginative plan about how to break into the think tank and steal the documents (through a fake fire and using fake firemen) it was never put into operation.

LIKE MOST PRESIDENTS, NIXON HAD HIS EYE ON THE 1972 REELECTION
campaign almost from the start of his first term. Planning intensified in
the spring of 1971. With the primary season less than a year away, the
war still going on, and demonstrators calling attention to that fact, the
president also intensified his efforts to obtain that elusive peace with
honor before election day 1972. It was thus in the spring of 1971 that
the administration began to move away from its demand for a mutual
withdrawal of troops from South Vietnam. The United States would
pull out but the North Vietnamese could stay. Now the chief sticking
point was Hanoi's demand that President Thieu must be removed from
office before it would agree to a cease-fire and a peace treaty.

With American troops becoming less of a factor on the battlefield
and with the antiwar movement in the streets and Democrats in Con-
gress maintaining their pressure on Nixon to end the war quickly,
Hanoi was encouraged to think it need not make any concessions on
Thieu to achieve total victory. As North Vietnamese negotiator Le Duc
Tho told Kissinger in September 1971, "I really don't know why I am
negotiating with you. I have just spent several hours with Senator
McGovern and your opposition will force you to give me what I
want."[17] On June 22 the Senate had passed a non-binding sense of the
Senate resolution stating, "It is the policy of the United States to ter-
minate at the earliest practicable date all military operations in
Indochina."

The president, however, was not bereft of cards to play, and one
of the most startling was the China card that he revealed on July 15.
Nixon announced that his esteemed national security advisor, Henry
Kissinger, had just returned from a secret mission to China where he
arranged a presidential visit for February. A visit to China belied
Nixon's hard-line hawkish image and also held out the hope that Bei-
jing might assist him in ending the Vietnam War.

In addition, the war against the antiwarriors intensified at home.
In August, when twenty-eight Catholic activists broke into a draft
board in Camden, New Jersey, the authorities were waiting for them.
The FBI informant in their midst was the person who advocated and
planned the activity. At the same time, the organized forces of dissent
were in more than the usual disarray, with the two major coalitions,
NPAC and PCPJ, almost as angry at one another as they were at Nixon.
Speaking generally of the problem, Tom Hayden wrote,

I began to realize in a rush how far many of us had strayed from the original disposition of the sixties. . . . In this sealed universe, social relationships were contained within organizations, language turned to jargon, disputes were elevated to doctrinal heights, paranoia replaced openness, and the struggle to change each other became a substitute for changing the world.[18]

The two coalitions, of which Hayden himself was not an active member, agreed to support a PCPJ demonstration on October 13, and NPAC demonstrations on November 6, with the PCPJ still rankling over the iron control exercised by NPAC in Washington on April 24. About 50,000 turned out nationwide for the "Evict Nixon" rallies on October 13, far fewer than expected in Washington, where 9,000 troops and policemen were on alert. On November 6, as many as 100,000 participated, with 25,000 in New York and 30,000 in San Francisco. More ominous for the movement than the relatively small turn-outs were the dwindling paid memberships in peace organizations. Although VVAW, a small organization was still growing, WILPF and CALC, for example, had each experienced between a 25 and 30 percent drop since 1969. Confronting small crowds and declining membership in peace organizations, one pacifist leader lamented, "We stand in the antechamber of a dying antiwar movement."[19]

Yet during that same period, 70 percent of the voters in Pittsfield, Massachusetts approved a resolution calling for an immediate cease fire and withdrawal of U.S. troops from Vietnam, Hollywood stars Jane Fonda and Donald Sutherland were attracting a good deal of attention on their nationwide FTA tour of appearances at coffee houses and other venues just outside military bases (FTA stood for either Free the Army or Fuck the Army depending upon the audience), but voters in San Diego rejected a referendum to keep the USS *Constellation* from leaving its port to go on duty in Vietnam. Home to the Pacific fleet, San Diego was a hotbed of antiwar activity, with a Stop Our Ship movement encouraging nine sailors to leave the *Kitty Hawk* to seek sanctuary in local churches. In November 1972, over 100 sailors from the *Constellation* participated in a strike that was considered the largest "mutiny" in the history of the modern American Navy.

The VVAW made a few headlines the day after Christmas in 1971 when sixteen members seized the Statue of Liberty, while several others briefly took over the Betsy Ross House in Philadelphia and another cadre invaded the South Vietnamese consulate in San Francisco. The

Statue of Liberty group wanted to declare the island independent and then recognize the government of North Vietnam. In addition, the People's Peace Treaty was still making the rounds, now endorsed by FOR, SANE, Common Cause, the ADA, the VVAW, and the AFSC. Finally, at the end of January 1972, four years to the month since Eartha Kitt embarrassed the First Lady in the White House, one of the wholesome, all-American Ray Coniff Singers unfolded a "Stop the Killing" banner in the middle of a White House concert.

The main problem with most of these activities, as was the case for the remainder of the war, was the lack of media interest. If there is little media interest, how does one influence the public and the administration when no one except the FBI knows what the movement is doing? The media lost its interest because, as we have seen, the many small activities that took place every day became normal and not "news." The only stories that made it past the editorial gatekeepers involved unusually violent or unlawful incidents; that sort of publicity was the last thing the antiwar movement needed in an election year when one of the candidates was running once again on a law-and-order platform. The media were only responding to the fact that by December 1971, only 15 percent of those polled thought the war was the most important problem the nation faced. That number had been deflated by the lack of media attention to the war and the movement. Reflecting the fact that the war had moved off page one into the interior of the newspapers, the PCPJ, whose leadership now came exclusively from liberal pacifists, decided early in 1972 to emphasize a multi-issue campaign revolving around the military-industrial complex, not only the war.

It faced formidable opposition from a president now in full-campaign mode, preparing for his historic, telegenic, and almost universally acclaimed visit to China in February. In January, he announced that Kissinger had been engaging in secret negotiations with North Vietnam's Le Duc Tho over the previous several years and that Washington's position had softened to a unilateral withdrawal of American troops in exchange for a ceasefire and a POW return. The main stumbling block, he informed the nation, was the Communists' insistence that there could be no settlement until President Thieu was removed from office. Now most observers had to conclude that the Communists were being unreasonable.

Nixon also announced the withdrawal of another 70,000 troops, which would leave only 69,000 in Vietnam by May 1. Ground combat had become almost exclusively a South Vietnamese task. What he did not say, which soon became apparent, was that he was intensifying the bombing campaign in order to pressure the North Vietnamese to make a concession on Thieu before the election. During the first three months of 1972, more bombs fell on North Vietnam than had fallen on that country during all of 1971, a fact that soon energized a Campaign to End the Air War. During the first four months of 1972, more than 3,500 members of CALC journeyed to Washington to lobby against the bombing. Concentrating on the air war, CALC also sponsored a radio program that ran six days a week on 300 stations.

At home, Nixon ordered the heat turned on those who opposed his policies. He complained about his critics, "We have done everything but offer surrender to the Communists. They want the United States to surrender to the Communists. . . . They are consciously giving aid and comfort to the enemy."[20] Although the media were no longer paying much attention to the movement, Nixon continued to harass and suppress its members to keep their activities from encouraging the Communists. He also used their allegedly unpatriotic behavior in his campaign against the Democrats.

He was even more angered at the Communists at home and abroad when on March 30, the North Vietnamese launched a major offensive that the South Vietnamese had to confront on the ground virtually alone; not in the air, of course, where the ongoing massive air campaign became even more massive. On April 15, Nixon ordered the bombing of Hanoi and Haiphong for the first time since 1968. This action produced a flurry of protests beginning with a rally of 1,000 in Washington on April 15, and violence on campuses including two hundred radicals storming Harvard's Center for International Affairs and protests in Maryland that led the governor to declare a state of emergency on April 20. One week after the bombing of Hanoi and Haiphong, at least 150 colleges experienced student strikes, many of which were accompanied by illegal or violent acts that fell under the then current rubric of "trashing."

NPAC hastily organized nationwide demonstrations on April 22 with 50,000 appearing in New York, 30,000 in San Francisco, and 20,000 in Los Angeles. Aside from the usual political figures such as David Dellinger, the New York event also featured former New York Yankee pitcher Jim Bouton. Even the normally apolitical League of Women Voters took a stand for the immediate withdrawal of American troops from Vietnam during the same period. But the polls supported Nixon's escalation of the air war by a 47–44 tally. For the majority, it only seemed fair since he was reacting to the North Vietnamese offensive that was launched after the United States could no longer offer effective opposition on the ground. The air war intensified still further during the summer—reaching an average of 300 strikes a day, with some sorties coming close to the previously off-limits Chinese border areas.

Buoyed by support for the bombing, Nixon went even further on May 8 when he announced the mining from the air of Hanoi's and Haiphong's harbors—an escalation that had been in the military's contingency plans for years but was resisted by the presidents for fear of domestic and international reaction. On the latter, it was a particularly sensitive matter since the president was due in Moscow later that month. Some in his entourage feared the Soviets would call off the summit and ruin Nixon's clever triangular diplomacy, but he guessed right. They were angry, but they had their own cards to play at the unprecedented meeting.

The movement's response to the mining escalation was escalation of its own. Students and other demonstrators in Santa Barbara, Boulder, and Chicago blockaded streets, while the city councils of Sacramento and Fort Wayne passed resolutions favoring an end to the war. Several of Kissinger's aides resigned because of the mining, Johnson aides Cyrus Vance, Paul Warnke, and Clark Clifford also expressed their opposition, and Jane Hart announced she would refuse to pay her federal taxes. In Los Angeles, all-American basketball player Bill Walton was arrested at a protest. When the president of Amherst College was arrested at a sit-in, he explained, "I speak out of frustration and despair. I do not think words will change the minds of the men in power who made these decisions."[21]

They certainly were not impressed by NPAC's and PCPJ's Washington rally on May 21 that drew only 15,000, at a time when 59 percent of those polled supported the mining. The organizers had expected a crowd of at least 50,000. At that rally endorsed also by ADA, SANE, WSP, and the Fifth Avenue Peace Parade Committee, Bella Abzug called for Nixon's impeachment. She followed up that announcement with the introduction of an impeachment resolution in the House, co-sponsored by William Fitts Ryan, another New York Democrat. Other activists soon announced the formation of a National Committee for

Impeachment. Little did they know that on June 17, a break-in at the Democratic headquarters in the Watergate complex in Washington would ultimately do the trick. They were far more interested in an unusual demonstration five days after the break-in at which 2,500 women and children, led by Joan Baez and WSP, formed a ring around Congress.

UNLIKE THE SITUATION IN 1968, MOST MEMBERS OF THE MOVEMENT expressed a clear choice for president in 1972. Democratic senator George McGovern owed his nomination in good measure to the movement. Because of the riots at the 1968 convention and the perception on the part of many liberal Democrats that their voices were not being heard, the party established a commission, headed by McGovern, to study the nomination process. The result was a series of rules put in place for the 1972 primary campaign and national convention that bent over backwards to make certain that women, blacks, young people, and others not in the party establishment received fair representation. Thus women constituted 38 percent of the delegates to the convention, young people 23 percent, blacks 15 percent, and overall, 39 percent of the delegates held postgraduate degrees. One party regular accurately observed, "I don't think these people represent the mainstream of the party."[22]

With new primaries in place and the convention looking decidedly unlike the one four years earlier, the Democrats selected their most liberal candidate to challenge Richard Nixon. McGovern was a liberal but not a radical as the president depicted him—overjoyed to have him as his opposition. Nixon's agents had worked through the primary season, employing a wide variety of illegal and extra-legal "dirty tricks," to weaken the chances of more centrist candidates like Edmund Muskie who posed more of a threat. During the campaign, McGovern, a longtime critic of the war, promised to stop the bombing and bring American troops home within ninety days of his election, making it sound as if he would do most anything to end the war. Nixon assaulted what he labeled McGovern's cowardly advocacy of "appeasement." In private discussions with McGovern in Paris in October 1971, a North Vietnamese diplomat had offered to help the senator's presidential candidacy by not permitting Nixon to make political gains in the peace talks.

Most of the leadership of the movement formally endorsed the senator's candidacy and encouraged their supporters to work on his campaign. Thus, members of such groups as BEM, SANE, WRL, and WILPF devoted a good deal of their energies to electoral politics during the summer and early fall of 1972, a fact that helped explain why the movement itself appeared to be relatively inactive during that period.

Tom Hayden and Jane Fonda did not work directly for McGovern, but their new Indochina Peace Campaign was devoted to getting rid of Richard Nixon. The two well-known activists toured the country armed with pamphlets and other informational material they shared with their audiences. Hayden, who was last seen supporting Weathermen-like activities, had moved back toward mainstream left-liberalism and even encouraged members in his group to wear American flags, just like the president and his aides. Jane Fonda was a mixed blessing for the movement. She had gone to North Vietnam in July where, speaking on Hanoi radio, she had urged a stop to the bombing. Moreover, she reported that the POWs had been treated quite well, and most damning, was photographed behind an antiaircraft gun that had been used to bring down American airplanes. Since that time, she has been remembered by many Americans as "Hanoi Jane." As late as April 2001, a picketer carried a sign outside a Fort Worth, Texas hall where she was speaking that read, "I'll forgive Jane when Jews forgive Hitler."

At the Republicans' convention in Miami in late August, 10,000 activists showed up to demonstrate against Nixon's reelection. The most disciplined among them were 1,000 members of the VVAW on their "Last Patrol." At the protesters' encampment in Flamingo Park, one could find along the "Ho Chi Minh Trail" tents promoting the Free Gays, Jesus Freaks, the People's Pot Park, SDS, Yippies, and a variant of that group, the Zippies. They promoted flag burnings, piss-ins, puke-ins, and a free marijuana rally.

Almost all of the groups present had been penetrated by intelligence agencies and, as usual by now, agents provocateurs encouraged violence that was met with tear gas, clubs, and arrests from the authorities. That is exactly what Nixon wanted to happen as he emphasized the violence of those who opposed him. His senior aides did not accept all of the schemes suggested by Watergate mastermind G. Gordon Liddy. He had proposed hiring professional killers to drug and kidnap movement leaders and drop them off in Mexico until the convention was over.

However, Liddy's crews were not able to stop three disabled members of VVAW, Ron Kovic, Bobby Muller, and Bill Wyman, from getting to the convention floor and briefly disrupting proceedings by chanting, "Stop the bombing, stop the war." Kovic wrote his memoirs soon after, *Born on the Fourth of July,* which was later made into a successful Hollywood film; Muller became head of Vietnam Veterans of America.

THE THREE VETS' CALL FOR AN END TO THE BOMBING AND AN END TO the war was answered, but not by George McGovern. During the summer of 1972, because of Nixon's heavy bombing, the lack of support from China and the Soviet Union, and the fear that a reelected Nixon might be even more hawkish than he had been in 1972, the North Vietnamese began to move on the chief stumbling block to peace, the disposition of the Saigon government. In October, they accepted a plan whereby Thieu would remain in power after a ceasefire until new elections were held under the auspices of a tripartite commission that would be established under the terms of the peace treaty. After Hanoi jumped the gun on announcing that an agreement had been reached, Henry Kissinger confirmed on October 26 "Peace is at hand." Thus, in their own October surprise, the Republicans had undercut George McGovern completely, since about the only thing he had going for him by that time was his promise to end the war. Nixon won the popular election in a landslide by a 61 to 38 percent margin and took all of the electoral votes except for those of Massachusetts and the District of Columbia.

Almost immediately after the election, he had to explain that peace was not quite at hand because the North Vietnamese had reneged on the agreement. That was not true. The South Vietnamese had rejected the agreement because it did not provide for the removal of North Vietnamese forces from their country after the ceasefire. Americans were never told that Saigon was the problem, and when negotiations broke off early in December, they assumed that the perfidious Communists had been cheating once again. Still, when Nixon decided to bomb them back to the peace table with massive B-52 attacks on Hanoi and

Haiphong from December 18 through December 30, many Americans were outraged once again by an apparent escalation. Fortunately for the president, the attacks occurred during the Christmas recess both on Capitol Hill and on college campuses. Of 73 senators polled, 45 expressed opposition to the bombing. One antiwar leader, Norma Becker, claimed that she was so horrified by the bombing that her hair began turning white during the period. There were scattered small demonstrations throughout the nation and strong condemnation from the media and foreign leaders, including the Swedish prime minister who likened the Nixon administration to the Nazis. But by the time Congress was in session and the colleges reopened in January, the bombing was over, Kissinger was talking to Le Duc Tho, and a peace treaty, looking very much like the October document, was initialed on January 23.

That peace was really at hand this time did not stop protesters from turning out for Nixon's second inauguration and for their own, second counterinaugural. Leonard Bernstein conducted Haydn's "Mass in the Time of War," for 20,000 on January 19. In a counterpoint, eleven members of the Philadelphia Orchestra refused to play for the president at the official concert that night. The next day, over 50,000 gathered at NPAC's "Out Now" rally at the Washington Monument, while during the inaugural parade itself, protesters along the route chanted and threw eggs, although they were not as numerous or as obstreperous as those in 1969. One man carried a placard that read, "Nixon's secret plan killed my son and 23,500 other GI's in Vietnam."[23]

NOTES

1. Nicosia, *Home to War*, 110–11.
2. Wells, *The War Within*, 495.
3. Small, *Covering Dissent*, 151.
4. Ibid., 152.
5. Ibid., 148.
6. Ibid., 150.
7. Ibid., 148.
8. Ibid, 153.
9. Wells, *The War Within*, 505.
10. Small, *Covering Dissent*, 156.
11. Small, *Johnson, Nixon, and the Doves*, 217.

12. Wells, *The War Within,* 502.

13. Small, *The Presidency of Richard Nixon,* 86.

14. Small, *Covering Dissent,* 160.

15. Colson, *Born Again,* 58.

16. Ambrose, *The Triumph of a Politician,* 447.

17. Vernon Walters, *Silent Missions* (Garden City, NJ: Doubleday, 1978), 518.

18. Hayden, *Reunion,* 435.

19. DeBenedetti, *An American Ordeal,* 320.

20. Hersh, *The Price of Power,* 486.

21. DeBenedetti, *An American Ordeal,* 330-31.

22. Peter N. Carroll, *It Seemed Like Nothing Happened: America in the 1970's* (New Brunswick, NJ: Rutgers University Press, 1990), 86.

23. Wells, *The War Within,* 564.

CHAPTER **Nine**

CONCLUSION

T HE ANTIWAR MOVEMENT, WHICH HAD NOT BEEN A SIGNIFICANT political factor in 1972, did not completely disappear on January 27, 1973, when the peace agreement was signed in Paris. From that point to the fall of Saigon to the Communists on April 30, 1975, in thousands of regional and national actions, activists rallied, marched, leafleted, and petitioned against further American assistance to the South Vietnamese and to the Cambodians who were engaged in a civil war with the communist Khmer Rouge. But the mass efforts paled in size and impact compared to those of the earlier period and, most importantly, the mainstream media were rarely interested. With the draft ended, no more American combat losses in Vietnam, a generation of activists in various stages of burnout, and the apparent end of the 1960s culture, it was difficult to attract large numbers of citizens to protest against U.S. policies in remote Southeast Asia.

As for the chances of re-escalation, although Richard Nixon had secretly promised President Thieu that if the North Vietnamese broke the agreement the United States would return to protect him, in 1973 he confronted a Democratic Congress that strongly opposed the recommitment of American troops or flyers to the war. Moreover, after his landslide victory in November 1972, things went rapidly downhill for the president who soon became embroiled in the Watergate crisis. In February 1973, several weeks after the Watergate burglars were found guilty, the House established a committee to investigate the break-in and related crimes. From that point to August 1974, when Nixon was forced to resign before he faced certain impeachment and removal from office, the nation was shocked by a series of ever more serious revelations about cover-ups, illegal activities, and corruption. Consumed by the crisis, the president was virtually powerless to help the South Vietnamese resist the Communists. Indeed, he later claimed that he could have saved his former allies from defeat had it not been for the way Watergate had crippled his presidency.

It is unlikely the United States could have done much to save South Vietnam. Both sides violated the terms of the peace agreement continually, with President Thieu foolishly going on the offensive in 1973, wildly squandering military supplies, which the United States later did not replace. With the Americans' withdrawal and a closing out of their aid programs, the South Vietnamese economy collapsed. Thieu's unpopular, corrupt, and inefficient government was no match for the North Vietnamese who began to make significant territorial gains late in 1974, preparatory to launching what became their final offensive early in the following year. Hanoi itself was surprised by how quickly the entire country collapsed after a brief, spirited defensive stand in April 1975.

Even if the domestic political situation had permitted re-intervention, American leaders might have been stopped by their judicial system had they tried to intervene. In the middle of 1973, the Supreme Court finally came close to ruling on the question of the constitutionality of at least one aspect of the war. Donald Dawson, an Air Force pilot, was court-martialed after he refused to participate in the bombing of Khmer Rouge-held areas in Cambodia. He challenged his court martial, claiming that such bombing, which continued after the end of the U.S. war in Vietnam, was illegal. On July 15, 1973, Judge Orin Judd of New York's Federal District Court issued an injunction against the bombing, contending that the grounds to justify it no longer existed. The government successfully appealed the injunction with the Supreme Court ready to act on the case, but by the time it reached the court, congressional pressure had forced the administration to stop the bombing, and the government dropped its case against Dawson.

After the Communists took over Saigon, which they renamed Ho Chi Minh City, New Yorkers gathered in Central Park for a rally that featured Joan Baez and Phil Ochs singing "The War is Over." Many in that teary-eyed crowd were convinced that the war was over because of their activities in the movement, which according to one leader had "become the focus of our lives . . . the center of everything."[1] They were certain they had compelled their government to stop escalating, to start talking, and to make peace eventually.

Not everyone agrees with that simple analysis of the impact of the antiwar movement. There are those who take the opposite tack—the antiwar movement prolonged the war because many Americans skeptical about the war were disturbed about associating themselves with what appeared to be repulsive hippies and unpatriotic radicals. One historian who concludes that in the movement there were "more clowns than heroes, more ignominy than virtue," cites Jerry Rubin who proclaimed, "We were fucking obnoxious and we dug every moment of it."[2]

In addition, some contend that had there been no antiwar movement to encourage the North Vietnamese, they would not have held out as long as they did. Bob Haldeman maintained that the movement "prolonged the war three-and-one-half years," by giving the Communists the false impression that they could rely on their "allies" in the United States to pressure their government to deliver the victory they could not win on the battlefield at the diplomatic table.[3]

A reasonable evaluation of the impact of the antiwar movement falls somewhere between that of activists who proudly claim credit for stopping the war and that of former U.S. officials who report that the only ones influenced by the doves were the Communists who held out longer than they would have because they misunderstood American politics. Whatever the overall evaluation, on at least two occasions, the antiwar movement affected presidential decision making for Vietnam.

The first was in November 1967 when the shock of the siege of the Pentagon helped to convince the president to launch a major public relations campaign to reassure Americans that the war was being won. The exaggerations of military progress that were remembered two months later during the early days of the Tet Offensive contributed significantly to the decline in support for a continuation of the president's policies in Vietnam and led him to make his epochal March 31, 1968 speech in which he eschewed both reelection and escalation.

Richard Nixon's decision not to retaliate when Hanoi did not respond to his July ultimatum by November 1, 1969, was even more directly related to the antiwar movement. On October 15, the president was surprised by the size and unique nature of the most impressive series of demonstrations of the period, the Moratorium. The participation in that event of many middle-class adults who engaged in dignified ceremonies and memorials helped to convince him that he would face considerable opposition were he to hit the North Vietnamese with the "savage blow" his aides were considering. Throughout his presidency, Nixon, who was convinced that he could achieve peace with honor through tough tactics, found himself restrained by the latent power of the movement and its allies in Congress and the media. If anything, the movement may have been more important under Nixon than Johnson. Although it could not stop Johnson from escalating from 1965 through 1968, it played a central role in making it difficult for Nixon to re-escalate from 1969 through 1971.

As for the contention that the only government listening to the antiwar movement was the one in Hanoi, even if that was the case, the Johnson and Nixon administrations' policies were affected by their perceptions of Hanoi's perceptions of the movement. Hanoi itself was encouraged by the movement but knew enough about American politics not to exaggerate its influence on the presidents. The movement did not lead to American military defeat by falsely encouraging the enemy. The failure of the American military to defeat the Communists quickly led to the growth of the antiwar movement and antiwar sentiment in the United States.

John Oakes, editor of the *New York Times* editorial page during much of the period, worried about the way the war "was tearing apart American society."[4] Although activist antiwar college students, hippies, the New Left, and revolutionary left together never constituted more than a minority of young people, they were disproportionately represented among the children of the establishment at leading colleges and universities. Their parents enjoyed disproportionate influence in government, the media, business, and other key institutions in American society. And they *were* worried—worried that their children would become or remain hippies, or end up in jail for participating in violent protests, or become drug addicts, or even revolutionaries.

To be sure, when these influential Americans, like the Wise Men in March 1968, concluded that the war had to be ended, they had evaluated the chances of a military victory, the global balance of power, the economy, and the impact of a withdrawal on their allies and enemies. But at least subconsciously, they also feared for the very future of the United States with so many of the "best and brightest" of their young people completely alienated by their government's policies in Southeast Asia. They had argued with them over the dinner table and at other family gatherings and those often bitter memories weighed heavily as they developed positions on the war in Vietnam.

The direct relationship between the movement and antiwar opinion in the United States is more difficult to establish. Undersecretary of State George Ball had predicted as early as the fall of 1964 that the limited war in Vietnam would end up like the limited war in Korea, one for which Americans demonstrated little patience. After several years of escalation without a victory, he warned that much of the population would tire of the effort and demand either all-out war or withdrawal. That is what seemed to have happened after the Tet Offensive when the light at the end of the tunnel was extinguished. But there is little doubt that arguments presented by antiwar spokespersons, heard and seen on television and read in newspapers and magazines, played some role in the development of public opinion. Considering the attention paid to the movement by media monitors in both administrations and the massive effort by U.S. intelligence agencies to penetrate and harass dovish organizations, it is clear that Johnson and Nixon thought that they were serious players in the battle for the hearts and minds of Americans. Both presidents discovered that in order to "win" the war in Vietnam, they had to win the war at home. By 1973 neither the antiwar movement nor the government could declare victory.

NOTES

1. Ronald Radosh, *Commies: A Journey through the Old Left, the New Left and the Leftover Left* (San Francisco: Encounter, 2001), 131.
2. DeGroot, *A Noble Cause*, 299, 306.
3. Small, *Johnson, Nixon, and the Doves*, 185.
4. Wells, *The War Within*, 260.

Bibliographical Essay

To understand the antiwar movement, one must first understand the Vietnam War. Two of the most balanced and respected studies are George C. Herring, *America's Longest War: The United States and Vietnam, 1950–1975* (New York: McGraw-Hill, 2002) and Robert Schulzinger, *A Time for War: The United States and Vietnam, 1941–1975* (New York: Oxford, 1997). Marilyn B. Young's *The Vietnam Wars, 1945–1990* (New York: HarperCollins, 1991) is a passionate survey from the Left. Among more recent general histories of value are Gerald J. DeGroot's thoughtful text, *A Noble Cause: America and the Vietnam War* (New York: Pearson, 2000), A. J. Langguth's lengthy journalistic account, *Our Vietnam: The War, 1954–1975* (New York: Simon and Schuster, 2000), and Robert Mann's equally lengthy *A Grand Delusion: America's Descent into Vietnam* (New York: Basic, 2001), which emphasizes the view from Congress. For the essential data in fewer than 100 pages, Mitchell Hall's *The Vietnam War* (New York: Pearson, 1999) is admirable. It would be helpful as well to examine John Morton Blum's *Years of Discord: American Politics and Society, 1961–1974* (New York: Norton, 1991) and David Farber and Beth Bailey, eds., *The Columbia Guide to America in the Sixties* (New York: Columbia University Press, 2001) to understand the backdrop of the war.

For the antiwar movement, one must first begin with an introduction to the political culture of the 1960s, Terry H. Anderson's colorful and kaleidoscopic *The Movement and the Sixties: Protest in America from Greensboro to Wounded Knee* (New York: Oxford University Press, 1995) and, for a global perspective, Arthur Marwick, *The Sixties: Cultural Revolution in Britain, France, Italy, and the United States, 1958–1974* (New York: Oxford University Press, 1998) before turning to the best history of the movement, Charles DeBenedetti with Charles Chatfield, *An American Ordeal: The Antiwar Movement of the Vietnam Era* (Syracuse: Syracuse University Press, 1990). Nancy Zaroulis and Gerald Sullivan in *Who Spoke Up? American Protest against the War in Vietnam, 1963–1975* (Garden City, NJ: Doubleday, 1984) offer a lively, if less scholarly, chronicle of the movement. Among others, still useful are journalist Thomas Powers's, *The War at Home* (New York: Grossman, 1973) and SWP leader Fred Halstead's memoir, *Out Now: A Participant's Account of the Movement against the Vietnam War in the United States* (New York: Pathfinder, 1978).

Give Peace a Chance: Exploring the Vietnam Antiwar Movement (Syracuse: Syracuse University Press, 1994), edited by Melvin Small and William D. Hoover, presents a wide variety of approaches to the movement. Rhodri Jeffreys-Jones looks at women, labor, blacks, and young people in *Peace Now: American Society and the Ending of the Vietnam War* (New Haven: Yale University Press, 1999) while Robbie Lieberman covers Communists in *The Strangest Dream: Communism, Anticommunism, and the U.S. Peace Movement, 1945–1963* (Syracuse: Syracuse University Press, 2000). In a controversial class by itself is Adam Garfinkle, *Telltale Hearts: The Origins and Impact of the Vietnam Antiwar Movement* (New York: St. Martin's, 1995), which is highly critical of the movement and those historians who evaluated it positively.

Useful documentary collections are Mary Susannah Robins, ed., *Against the Vietnam War: Writings by Activists* (Syracuse: Syracuse University Press, 1999) and Louis Menashe and Ronald Radosh, eds., *Teach-ins USA: Reports, Opinions, Documents* (New York: Praeger, 1967). Melvin Small examines the impact of the movement on the decision makers in *Johnson, Nixon, and the Doves* (New Brunswick: Rutgers University Press, 1988) and Tom Wells does the same in *The War Within: America's Battle over Vietnam* (Berkeley: University of California Press, 1994). Both authors interviewed scores of administration officials to determine how the movement affected them. Those officials were concerned about how the media treated the doves, a subject studied by Small in *Covering Dissent: The Media and the Antiwar Movement* (New Brunswick: Rutgers University Press, 1994).

For specific groups see Mitchell K. Hall, *Because of Their Faith: CALCAV and Religious Opposition to the War in Vietnam* (New York: Columbia University Press, 1990), Amy Swerdlow, *Woman Strike for Peace* (Chicago: University of Chicago Press, 1993), and Michael Ferber and Staughton Lynd, *The Resistance* (Boston: Beacon, 1971).

Among those who wrote about their experiences in the movement are Todd Gitlin, *The Sixties: Years of Hope and Days of Rage* (New York: Bantam, 1987), which is more of a monograph than a memoir; Tom Hayden, *Reunion: A Memoir* (New York: Random House, 1988); Abbie Hoffman, *Soon to be a Major Motion Picture* (New York: G. P. Putnam, 1980); antiwar vet Ron Kovic's *Born on the Fourth of July* (New York: Simon and Schuster, 1976); David Dellinger, *More Power Than We Know: The People's Movement toward Democracy* (Garden City, NJ: Doubleday, 1975); David Harris, *Dreams Die Hard* (New York: St. Martin's, 1982); and Ronald Radosh's critical *Commies: A Journey through the Old Left, the New Left and the Leftover Left* (San Francisco: Encounter, 2001).

For campus studies, Kenneth J. Heineman has written two valuable books, with the first—*Campus Wars: The Peace Movement at American State Universities in the Vietnam Era* (Albany: State of New York University Press, 1993)—more balanced than the lively critique, *Put Your Bodies upon the Wheels: Student Revolt in the 1960's* (Chicago: Ivan Dee, 2001). Heineman also wrote an article in the interesting collection edited by Marc Jason Gilbert, *The Vietnam War on Campus: Other Voices, More Distant Drums* (Westport: Praeger, 2001). The standard SDS history remains Kirkpatrick Sale, *SDS: Ten Years toward a Revolution* (New York: Vintage, 1973). For events at two of the most politically active campuses, see W. J. Rorabaugh, *Berkeley at War: The 1960's* (New York: Oxford University Press, 1989) and Tom Bates, *RADS: The 1970 Bombing of the Army Math Research Center at the University of Wisconsin and Its Aftermath* (New York: HarperCollins, 1992). Roger Rapoport and Laurence J. Kirshbaum, *Is the Library Burning?* (New York: Random House, 1969) is a revealing contemporary account.

For the draft and how young Americans dealt with it, see Lawrence M. Baskir and William A. Strauss, *Chance and Circumstance: The Draft, the War and the Vietnam Generation* (New York: Knopf, 1978). Some chose conscientious objection as seen in James Tollefson's *The Strength Not to Fight* (Boston: Little Brown, 1993). Dissenting vets are the subject of Andrew E. Hunt, *The Turning: A History of the Vietnam Veterans against the War* (New York: New York University Press, 1999) and the longer journalistic account, Gerald Nicosia, *Home to War: The Vietnam Veterans Movement* (New York: Crown, 2001). David Cortright, *Soldiers in Revolt: The American Military Today*

(Garden City, NJ: Doubleday, 1975) deals with insubordination and mutiny in the active-duty military.

How the American intellectual community dealt with war is covered by Robert R. Tomes, *Apocalypse Then: American Intellectuals and the Vietnam War* (New York: New York University Press, 1998), David Levy, *The Debate over Vietnam* (Baltimore: Johns Hopkins University Press, 1991), and Sandy Vogelsgang, *The Long Dark Night of the Soul: The American Intellectual Left and the Vietnam War* (New York: Harpers, 1974). Intellectuals were among the targets of the intelligence agencies as seen in James Kirkpatrick, *Assault on the Left: The FBI and the Sixties Antiwar Movement* (Westport: Praeger, 1997). One intellectual who was particularly targeted was the Pentagon Papers' Daniel Ellsberg, whose story is told in Tom Wells's lively, *Wild Man of the Left: The Life and Times of Daniel Ellsberg* (New York: Palgrave, 2001).

Lyndon Johnson's responses to the movement are noted in Lloyd Gardner, *Pay Any Price: Lyndon Johnson and the Wars for Vietnam* (Chicago: Ivan Dee, 1995), while Jeffrey Kimball is the best source for Nixon in *Nixon's Vietnam War* (Lawrence: University Press of Kansas, 1998), supplemented by Larry Berman, *No Peace, No Honor: Nixon, Kissinger, and Betrayal in Vietnam* (New York: Free Press, 2001). Prominent antiwar senators are the subjects of Joseph A. Palermo, *In His Own Right: The Political Odyssey of Senator Robert F. Kennedy* (New York: Columbia University Press, 2001) and William C. Berman, *William Fulbright and the Vietnam War: The Dissent of a Political Realist* (Kent, OH: Kent State University Press, 1988).

Index

Hart, Phil, 114
Hartke, Vance, 143
Harvard University, 49, 105, 109,
124, 152
Hatfield, Mark, 134
Hawk, David, 106, 107
Hayakawa, S. I., 87
Hayden, Tom: on conflict between
coalitions, 149–50; at Democratic
National Convention (1968), 97;
on hippies and yippies, 80; indict-
ment of, 106; in Indochina Peace
Campaign, 155; meetings with
North Vietnamese, 40–41, 67; on
Nixon, 120; *The Other Side,* 40;
public recognition of, 32; SDS
and, 29; as spokesperson, 29; on
student activists, 87
Heard, Alexander, 124
Hellman, Lillian, 43
Hersey, John, 43
Hershey, Lewis, 33, 109
Herz, Alice, 21
Heschel, Abraham, 51, 90, 105
Hester, Hugh, 72
Heston, Charlton, 43
Hickel, Walter, 124
Hippies, emergence of, 79–81
Hiroshima Day, 12, 14
Ho Chi Minh, 9–10, 111
Hoffa, James, 63
Hoffman, Abbie: Agnew and, 103;
on antiwar movement, 1; at
Democratic National Convention
(1968), 97; indictment of, 106; at
New Mobe demonstration (1969),
115; at Washington rally (1967),
78; and Yippie Party, 80
Honeywell Corporation, 132
Honor America Day, 128
Honorary degrees, 44
Hoover, J. Edgar, 114, 128–29
Hope, Bob, 128
House Committee on Un-American
Activities (HUAC), 7, 61
Howe, Irving, 8, 77
"How to Lower Your Blood Pres-
sure" (pamphlet), 63
HUAC. *See* House Committee on
Un-American Activities

Hubbard, Orville, 48
Humphrey, Hubert: confrontation
with protesters, 49; in 1968 presi-
dential election, 93, 96–101
Hunt, Howard, 148
Huppe, Kathy, 132–33
Huston Plan, 102, 129

I
Immolation. *See* Self-immolation
Indochina Peace Campaign, 155
Intellectuals, criticism of society by,
8–9
Intelligence agencies: civil liberties
violations by, 61, 101–2, 129;
under Nixon, 101–2, 119, 129,
155
Interfaith Committee to Set the
Date, 132
Interfaith Peace Commission, 44
Internal Revenue Service (IRS), 102,
129
International Days of Protest: in
1965, 32–33, 34; in 1966, 46
Interreligious Committee on Viet-
nam, 51
IRS. *See* Internal Revenue Service
Israel, 52

J
Jackson State College, 123
Japan, 9
Jeannette Rankin Brigade, 57
Johns Hopkins University, 24, 124
Johnson, Lady Bird, 43
Johnson, Luci, 42
Johnson, Lyndon: in Australia/New
Zealand, 48; and bombing campaign (1965-1968), 19, 20–21, 91;
and bombing pause (1966), 40;
Bundy and, 23; on Communists in
antiwar movement, 61–62; confrontations with protesters, 42–43,
48–49, 92; Congress and, 25; early
views on Vietnam, 13; Great Society programs of, 25; and ground
combat, 30; Gulf of Tonkin Resolution by, 14; impact of antiwar
movement on, 92–93, 161–62;
Johns Hopkins speech by (1965),

32366859R00113

Made in the USA
San Bernardino, CA
04 April 2016